Management Education
and Automation

Due to automation, nearly half of the jobs will vanish over the next two decades in the US. However, the problem is not confined to any particular country. Management educators in higher education are faced with two fundamental questions: (a) how we prepare our students for new required technology competencies when conducting international business and (b) how we work with new technologies to prepare our students. While the next generation of employees requires competencies in working with artificial intelligence relying on data analytics, the emergence of artificial intelligence and new technologies in augmenting teaching is changing the nature of higher education across the globe.

Management Education and Automation explores international management education in light of exponential development of artificial intelligence, big data, demographic shifts, expansion of robotic utilization in many economic sectors, aging populations and negative population growth in developed economies, multipolar international political systems, migration patterns, and fundamental shifts in individual and social interactions via digital media.

It shows the latest state of knowledge on the topic and will be of interest to researchers, academics, policymakers, and students in the fields of international business and management, globalization, management education, and management of technology and innovation.

Hamid H. Kazeroony is a Senior Contributing Faculty Member for the PhD Management Program at Walden University, Extraordinary Professor at N.W. University, South Africa, and a Professor at Minnesota State Colleges and Universities, US.

Denise Tsang (Cert Ed, BA, PhD, FRSA) is a Lecturer at the University of Reading and Certified Management and Business Educator of the Chartered Association of Business Schools in the UK.

Routledge Advances in Management and Business Studies

For more information about this series, please visit: www.routledge.com/
Routledge-Advances-in-Management-and-Business-Studies/book-series/
SE0305

Management Education and Automation

Edited by
Hamid H. Kazeroony and Denise Tsang

Routledge
Taylor & Francis Group

NEW YORK AND LONDON

First published 2022
by Routledge
605 Third Avenue, New York, NY 10158

and by Routledge
2 Park Square, Milton Park, Abingdon, Oxon OX14 4RN

Routledge is an imprint of the Taylor & Francis Group, an informa business

Library of Congress Cataloging-in-Publication Data
Names: Kazeroony, Hamid H., editor. | Tsang, Denise, 1965– editor.
Title: Management education and automation / edited by
Hamid H. Kazeroony and Denise Tsang.
Description: Abingdon, Oxon; New York, NY: Routledge, 2022. |
Series: Routledge advances in management and business studies |
Includes bibliographical references and index.
Identifiers: LCCN 2021009454 (print) | LCCN 2021009455 (ebook) |
ISBN 9780367861117 (hardback) | ISBN 9781032061085 (paperback) |
ISBN 9781003017707 (ebook)
DOI: 10.4324/9781003017707
Subjects: LCSH: Management–Study and teaching. |
Artificial intelligence. | Automation.
Classification: LCC HD30.4.M3274 2022 (print) |
LCC HD30.4 (ebook) | DDC 658.0071/1–dc23
LC record available at https://lccn.loc.gov/2021009454
LC ebook record available at https://lccn.loc.gov/2021009455

ISBN: 978-0-367-86111-7 (hbk)
ISBN: 978-1-032-06108-5 (pbk)
ISBN: 978-1-003-01770-7 (ebk)

Typeset in Sabon
by Newgen Publishing UK

Contents

Figures

Tables

Editors

Hamid H. Kazeroony is a human resource professional, certified SPHR, and SHRM-SCP. He earned his BA and MA in political science from California State University Pomona and Fullerton. He earned his MBA in International Management and his Doctorate in Organizational Leadership from the University of Phoenix, Arizona. He is a Senior Contributing Faculty at Walden University, PhD Program, US, Appointed Extraordinary Professor at N.W University, South Africa, Chair of Gender and Diversity in Organization, EURAM. His research reflects his interest in how production and diversity methods impact organizational leaders, institutions, values, and ethics, as manifested in his recent editorial contributions to a wide range of academic books and journals. He is a reviewer at the *Africa Journal of Management*, EURAM, and AOM conferences.

Denise Tsang (Cert Ed, BA, PhD, FRSA) is a Lecturer at the University of Reading and Certified Management and Business Educator of the Chartered Association of Business Schools in the UK. She gained a PhD scholarship in the Department of Economics in Reading in 1994 and has obtained research grants from the China Europe International Business School, the British Academy, the Japan Foundation Endowment Fund, and the Leverhumle Trust. Her research interests include strategic organizational issues from internal and external perspectives. She has written over 40 articles, 4 book chapters, and 4 monographs. She has also coedited the *Routledge Companion to International Management Education*. She is an experienced foundation, undergraduate, and postgraduate lecturer and has successfully supervised eight doctoral students. She is a regular speaker in the Annual Global Congress of Knowledge Economy.

Contributors

James Baba Abugre is an associate professor of Human Resource Management at the University of Ghana Business School and a senior consultant with the Corporate Support Group – Ghana. He is the executive secretary of the Academy of African Business and Development (AABD). He holds a PhD in International Human Resource Management from Swansea University in the UK, an MPhil in Human Resource Management, and an MA in Communication Studies from the University of Ghana. He teaches and researches human resource management and development in multinational and local organizations, cross-cultural and comparative management, and organizational and interpersonal communication. His research works have been published in leading management and international journals.

Aneta Aleksander holds a Doctor of Philosophy (PhD). She is an assistant professor at the Silesian University of Technology, Faculty of Organization and Management, Vice Editor-in-Chief of *Organization and Management Scientific Quarterly*. Her research is focused on international management, marketing, organizational identity, transfer of technology, innovations management, the role of business support organizations, internationalization of small- and medium-sized enterprises (SMEs), organizational behaviors and leadership, diversity management, and Industry 4.0. She is a member of the Academy of Management and a business expert and regional manager in the Enterprise Europe Network – one of the largest networks funded by the European Commission to facilitate SMEs' internationalization processes. The author of several publications in the fields mentioned above and the author of audits and numerous consultancy services and innovation audits.

Anita Asiwome Adzo Baku holds a Doctor of Philosophy (PhD) in Management from the Putra Business School in Malaysia and is currently a senior lecturer in the Department of Public Administration and Health Services Management at the University of Ghana Business School, Legon. She teaches health services management courses, and her research covers health management, health insurance, social insurance, occupational safety, and health marketing health services. Her writings cover book chapters and journal articles. She is also a reviewer for some international journals in health, social policy, and occupational safety and health.

Obi Berko Obeng Damoah is a senior lecturer in the Department of Organization and Human Resource Management, University of Ghana Businesses School. He holds a PhD in Strategy and International Business from Cardiff Metropolitan University, UK. He has published in high impact peer-reviewed journals (e.g., *International Journal of Manpower, Critical Perspectives in International Business, African Journal of Management*). He is a best paper Award Winner at one of AFAM's Biennial International Conferences hosted at Ethiopia, Addis Ababa in January 2018. Since August 2019, he has been serving as the African representative of the Strategic Management Division of the Academy of Management.

Guy Ellis (BA, BCom, MSc) has been recognized as one of the 101 top employee engagement influencers globally since 2016. He is the managing director of CourageousWorkplaces Limited. Established in 2003, CourageousWorkplaces has extensive experience in helping professionals, particularly those in HR, compliance, and finance roles, to become more productive and effective in the workplace. Guy has recently launched GenZ Insight (www.genzinsight.com) with two colleagues, which is a business that supports GenZ employees, their managers and leaders in integrating the newest generation to enter the workforce. Guy has coauthored *GenZ insight: How to become a GenZ Magnet, Tales of Talent: A Modern Fable for Today's Managers*, contributed to *Talent Management of Knowledge Workers*, and coedited *The Routledge Companion to International Management Education*.

Huda Masood is a doctoral candidate and a researcher at the School of Human Resource Management, York University, Toronto, Ontario. She is also a student relations liaison at the Canadian Society of Industrial and Organizational Psychology. Her research interests include the motivation and consequences of proactive behaviors at work, organizational justice, and workplace stress. Huda is also passionate about the research on the intersection of the dark side of leadership and human resource management functions. She has showcased her work at several local and international outlets such as the Academy of Management, Midwest Academy Management, Administrative Sciences Association of Canada, and Global Labour Research Conference.

Meiko Murayama earned her PhD from the University of Surrey, UK, on urban regeneration and tourism in England. She teaches business at the University of Reading, UK, and regularly conducts research and teaching at Akita International University, Japan, as a visiting researcher. She has published a wide range of topics, including blended learning and gamification in business education using ICT, revitalization through tourism development in rural and urban areas, and recently on cruise tourism in Japan. She has taught various subjects, including marketing, business principles, tourism management, and ethical tourism planning in Japan and the UK as an associate professor and senior lecturer. She emphasizes ethics and sustainability in all her teaching.

Brighton Nyagadza is a Doctor of Philosophy (PhD) (Marketing Management) finalist at Midlands State University (MSU), Zimbabwe, and a full-time digital marketing lecturer and Acting Chairperson for Supply Chain Management and Marketing Management Department at Marondera University of Agricultural Sciences and Technology (MUAST), Zimbabwe. He is an associate of The Chartered Institute of Marketing (CIM), UK, Power Member of the Digital Marketing Institute (DMI), Ireland, Dublin, and Full Member of the Marketers Association of Zimbabwe (MAZ). His interdisciplinary research expertise revolves on digital marketing, strategic management, entrepreneurship, corporate storytelling for branding, and marketing metrics.

Toyoko Sato is an external lecturer in the Department of Management, Society, and Communications of Copenhagen Business School. She holds a BA from the University of Wisconsin, Madison, an MA from Roskilde University, and a PhD in Organization and Management Studies from Copenhagen Business School. She received the Best Student Paper Award from the Management History division at the 2010 Academy of Management (AOM) Annual Meeting. Sato is a 2020 Fetzer Scholar for the Management, Spirituality, and Religion (MSR) Interest Group of the Academy. Publications include "Creative destruction and music industry in the age of diversity" (2014), "Organizational identity and symbioticity: Parco as an urban medium" (2010), and coauthor for "MSR founders' narrative and content analysis of scholarly papers: 2000–2015". She contributed to the *Routledge Companion to International Business* (Tsang, Kazeroony, & Ellis, 2013) with "Ethics and social responsibility in international business."

Foreword

The aim of this book is twofold: it refocuses the conversation about the required skill sets for those who manage global enterprises locally or globally; and it redefines the domain of international management in light of changes from traditional conversation about cross-border cultural management to the continuous changes in processes resulting from organizational interactions with the open system requiring realignment of international manager's approaches to new realities.

This book aims to help management educators reorient themselves to effectively address (a) the nature of change in the workplace based on the introduction of artificial intelligence (AI) and big data and (b) grasp the effects of multipolar international political system on deglobalization and glocalization of economies in providing the correct insights and pathways to ensure their students' success after graduation.

Due to automation, nearly half of the jobs will vanish over the next two decades in the US (Selingo, 2017). However, the problem is not confined to any country. Therefore, management educators in the higher education are faced with two fundamental questions: (a) how we prepare our students for new required technology competencies when conducting international business and (b) how we work with new technologies to prepare our students. While the next generation of employees requires competencies in working with AI relying on data analytics (New-Collar Jobs, 2018), the emergence of AI and new technologies in augmenting teaching is changing the nature of higher education across the globe (Popenici & Kerr, 2017).

Others have summarized the state of international management education (IME) and re-examined it with a critical approach, addressing the nature and relevance of different international management and business disciplines taught while attempting to arrive at consensus about what IME means in the light of globalization, touching on impact of innovations (Tsang, Kazeroony, & Ellis, 2013). This book will explore IME in light of exponential development of AI, big data, demographic shifts, expansion of robotic utilization in many economic sectors, aging populations and negative population growth in developed economies, multipolar international political systems, migration patterns, and fundamental shifts in individual and social interactions via digital media. Also, this proposal contextualizes cultural intelligence, positive energy, and social responsibility within the context of IME. Finally, this book will examine the future meaning of global IME in the light of deglobalization and glocalization.

While the current employees have begun to panic about the loss of their jobs based on the introduction of automation, teachers have begun dreading the shift from the traditional way of teaching to leveraging technology. A plethora of opportunities exists for the current and future employees to augment their competencies and become proficient knowledge workers, avoiding layoffs (Davenport & Kirby, 2015). By mastering few principles, teachers can shift from traditional to integrating automation in preparing future students. In teaching, management educators must determine the nature of interactions between students and machines, creating learning outcomes through connecting students to curriculum design, resources as library, social life, and instructions (Ozbey, Karakose, & Ucar, 2016). Several successful experiments have shown a large body of students interacting with a single instructor, utilizing AI and big data to reduce the need for instructors (Goes, 2016). Also, efforts by colleagues like Thrun's resignation from Stanford to teach free online courses, Khan's academy, and massive open online courses (MOOC) have added new layers of digital utilization to reduce costs, liberate monopoly on knowledge creation, and allow mass participation (DeMillo, 2015), as did the Protestant Reformation movement from 1517 to 1648, shifting the control from centralized authorities to the public.

Part I lays the groundwork about envisioning the future based on the current trends in societal, industrial, and technological in light of the drive for sustainability. Part II explores the skill gaps for employability, as evidenced by generational gap, Industry 4.0, and the curricula used in academia. Part III reviews some examples the current educational disparities between institutions based on policies and resources in providing technology integrated curricula that can prepare students for the future job market. Part IV provides a framework for planning, organizing, leading, and implementing systematic processes in reorienting the international teaching paradigm for the future.

Hamid H. Kazeroony

References

Gose, B. (2016, October 28). When the teaching assistant is a robot. *Chronicle of Higher Education*, pp. B10–B11.

Davenport, T. H., & Kirby, J. (2015). Beyond automation: strategies for remaining gainfully employed in an era of very smart machines. *Harvard Business Review*, 93(6), p. 58.

DeMillo, R. A. (2015, September 18). Gatekeepers no more: colleges must learn a new role. *Chronicle of Higher Education*, p. 16.

New-Collar Jobs. (2018). *TD: Talent Development, 72*(2), p. 12.

Ozbey, N., Karakose, M., & Ucar, A. (2016). The determination and analysis of factors affecting to student learning by artificial intelligence in higher education. *2016 15th International Conference on Information Technology Based Higher Education and Training (ITHET)*, p. 1. doi:10.1109/ITHET.2016.7760740

Popenici, S. & Kerr, S. (2017). Exploring the impact of artificial intelligence on teaching and learning in higher education. *Research and Practice in Technology Enhanced Learning, 12*(1), pp. 1–13. doi:10.1186/s41039-017-0062-8

Selingo, J. J. (2017). Are colleges preparing students for the automated future of work? *The Washington Post*.

Tsang, D., Kazeroony, H. H., & Ellis, G. (2013). *The Routledge Companion to International Management Education*. London: Routledge.

Part I
Envisioning the Future

1 Framing Automation and Management Education

Hamid H. Kazeroony

Background

Due to automation, nearly half of the jobs will vanish over the next two decades in the US (Selingo, 2017). However, the problem is not confined to any country. Therefore, management educators in higher education are faced with two fundamental questions: (a) how we prepare our students for the new required technology competencies and (b) how we work with new technologies to prepare our students. While the next generation of employees requires competencies in working with artificial intelligence (AI) relying on data analytics (New-Collar Jobs, 2018), the emergence of AI and new technologies in augmenting teaching is changing the nature of higher education (Popenici & Kerr, 2017). As management educators, we must address the nature of change in the workplace based on the introduction of AI, big data, decision-making automation, and offering services and products using robotics to help ensure employment for our graduates and learn to teach with it.

While the current employees have begun to panic about the loss of their jobs based on the introduction of AI, teachers have started dreading the shift from traditional teaching to leveraging technology. A plethora of opportunities exist for current and future employees to augment their competencies and become proficient knowledge workers, avoiding layoffs (Davenport & Kirby, 2015). Teachers mastering a few principles can shift from traditional to integrating AI in preparing future students.

In teaching, management educators must determine the nature of interactions between students and machines, creating learning outcomes through connecting students to curriculum design, resources as library, social life, and instructions (Ozbey et al., 2016). Several successful experiments have shown students' large body interacting with a single instructor, utilizing AI and big data to reduce instructors' need (Gose, 2016). Thrun's resignation from Stanford to teach free online courses, the creation of Khan's academy, and the opening of massive open online courses have added new layers of digitization, reduced costs, and conquered the monopoly over the knowledge creation channels (DeMillo, 2015). The movement echoes the Protestant Reformation movement from 1517 to 1648, shifting the Church's control to the masses. We will examine the role of automation, AI, and management education in preparing future graduates for employability. However, we must first address the current automation efforts and their possible impact on future graduates' future employability from the Higher Education Institutions (HEIs).

Several recent developments have shown an acceleration of automation across all industries, economic sectors, and societies. A recent survey revealed that 85% of chief executive officers would be spending more on automation of companies ranging from 1,000 to 10,000 employees in every aspect of their operations by 2021 (Castellanos, 2019). Therefore, reducing the need for some employees who require a different skill set for working and creating new automation. Homes are becoming smarter, combining residents' biographical information, automating home functions (Gamerman, 2019). Companies are investing considerable money in retraining many employees on machine learning. For example, Amazon has planned to spend $7,000 on each of the 100,000 employees by 2026 for machine learning (Cutter, 2019). The mechanical technicians who traditionally used wrenches and screwdrivers now utilize biometric information, leveraging technology to do their work (Shah, 2019). There is already a concentrated effort to introduce robotics to children as early as preschoolers and understand the psychological effects of robot interactions with children (Shellenbarger, 2019). As the pandemics began, a cultural shift began taking hold in the workplace, away from the office cubicles to the home environment (Shah, 2020). The year 2021 appears to be rife with exponential proliferation of cloud computing, more machine learning, utilization of data analytics by emergency personnel to help prevent disasters and expand quantum computing in more connected devices and people (Loftus, 2020). Finally, the realization of a sustainable society (SDG) to incorporate digital advances relies on the fourth industrial revolution. Industry 4.0 (I4.0) has started to take hold in some countries to balance the human needs versus economic systems, creating Society 5.0 (Fukuyama, 2018). These are simply a few examples of automation, requiring a fundamental shift in HEIs shifting its approach to management education to provide students with different skill sets for the new job market.

At this critical juncture, HEIs face several challenges in retooling themselves with new approaches to prepare the current generation of students for workforce readiness. In the complex integrated work competences, almost all manual and mechanical functions have been discontinuing and replaced with new robotics and automated competences, requiring new skillsets (McKinley, 2020). Managers need understanding and training addressing employees' cognitive challenges induced by changes from Industry 4.0 (Schneider & Sting, 2020). The nature of professional organizations such as law firms and financial organizations have changed, requiring different approaches to managing them (Kronblad, 2020). Digitalization has changed the nature of relationships between individuals, work, organizations, and society, changing how employees work and communicate (Wang et al., 2020). With the rise of AI, organizations must create a trusting bond between employees and AI, relying on each other to meet organizational objectives (Glikson & Woolley, 2020). The reliance on big data has changed the nature and span of managerial control, creating a dilemma for managers walking a tight rope between coercive approaches and understanding appropriate leadership approaches in managing people (Schafheitle et al., 2020). The SDG, digitalization, and I4.0 have created changes at macro, meso, and microlevels. The changes require different HEI approaches, addressing retooling the management education programs graduates with different skillsets for employability and to thrive in the new environment.

Chapters Overview

To lay the ground, we will first address the macro level. Society 5.0, Murayama, uses Japan's government approach to lay the foundations for applying I4.0, digitizing, and balancing economic needs for production with human needs, employment, and wellbeing. At the meso level, first, Nyagadza explains the fourth industrial revolution (I4.0), its consequences, and its impact on the future of work and social dynamics. Second, Sato explores how the intersectionality of science, technology, and society studies in production forces has led to fundamental changes that require a new approach to working in a new environment.

Next, turning our attention to HEIs, Ellis examines the training and development within the organizational context at the microlevel, addressing the differences based on generational needs. Aleksander explores the impact of Industry 4.0 on future leaders. Masood, taking a broad view of HEIs, examines the boundaryless careers and the role of HEIs in offering students the necessary tools to make them employable. Damoah and Baku provide a comparative perspective of the resources, explaining how education prepares students for future employability and poses geographic challenges based on digital divides. Abugre, offering a case from Sub-Saharan Africa, examines integrating AI into curricula for effective teacher–learner interaction.

In the last part, connecting the dots, Kazeroony offers a critical examination of how we should reshape the future of management education. In this examination, Kazeroony reviews the macro, the meso, and the microlevel developments requiring rethinking the future management education. He offers a set of a concrete plans of action for effective management education to address the automation trends.

References

Castellanos, S. (April 11, 2019). Intuit CIO: Be strategic about the bots you build. *Wall Street Journal.*

Cutter, C. (July 11, 2019). Amazon to retrain a third of its US workforce. *Wall Street Journal.*

Davenport, T. H., & Kirby, J. (2015). Beyond automation: Strategies for remaining gainfully employed in an era of very smart machines. *Harvard Business Review, 93*(6), pp. 58–65.

DeMillo, R. A. (2015, September 18). Gatekeepers no more: Colleges must learn a new role. *Chronicle of Higher Education.* p. 16.

Fukuyama, M. (2018). Society 5.0: Aiming for a new human-centered society. *Japan Spotlight, 27*, pp. 47–50.

Gamerman, A. (June 20, 2019). Home is where they know your name (and face, hands and fingerprints). *Wall street Journal.*

Glikson, E., & Woolley, A. W. (2020). Human trust in artificial intelligence: Review of empirical research. *Academy of Management Annals, 14*(2), pp. 627–660. https://doi.org/10.5465/annals.2018.0057

Gose, B. (2016, October 28). When the teaching assistant is a robot. *Chronicle of Higher Education.* pp. B10–B11.

Kronblad, C. (2020). How digitalization changes our understanding of professional service firms. *Academy of Management Discoveries, 6*(3), pp. 436–454.

Loftus, T. (December 17, 2020). Amazon's chief technology officer shares his predictions for 2021. *Wall Street Journal.*

McKinley, W. (2020). Doomsdays and new dawns: Technological discontinuities and competence ecosystems. *Academy of Management Perspectives, 34*(4), pp. 425–433.

New-Collar Jobs. (2018). *TD: Talent Development, 72*(2), p. 12.

Ozbey, N., Karakose, M., & Ucar, A. (2016). The determination and analysis of factors affecting to student learning by artificial intelligence in higher education. *2016 15th International Conference on Information Technology Based Higher Education and Training (ITHET)*, p. 1. doi:10.1109/ITHET.2016.7760740

Popenici, S. & Kerr, S. (2017). Exploring the impact of artificial intelligence on teaching and learning in higher education. *Research & Practice in Technology Enhanced Learning, 12*(1), pp. 1–13. doi:10.1186/s41039-017-0062-8

Schafheitle, S., Weibel, A., Ebert, I., Kasper, G., Schank, C., & Leicht-Deobald, U. (2020). No stone left unturned? Toward a framework for the impact of datafication technologies on organizational control. *Academy of Management Discoveries, 6*(3), pp. 455–487.

Schneider, P. & Sting, F. J. (2020). Employees' perspectives on digitalization-induced change: Exploring frames of industry 4.0. *Academy of Management Discoveries, 6*(3), pp. 406–435. http://doi.org/10.5465/amd.2019.0012

Selingo, J. J. (2017). Are colleges preparing students for the automated future of work? *The Washington Post.*

Shah, A. (August 11, 2019). Otis elevator's bet on technology. *Wall Street Journal.*

Shah, A. (March 12, 2020). Working remotely requires cultural change, executives say. *Wall Street Journal.*

Shellenbarger, S. (August 26, 2019). Why we should teach kids to call the robot 'It'. *Wall Street Journal.*

Wang, B., Liu, Y., & Parker, S. K. (2020). How does the US of information communication technology affect individuals? A work design perspective. *Academy of Management Annals, 14*(2), pp. 695–725. https://doi.org/10.5465/annals.2018.0127

2 Society 5.0 Transformation

Digital Strategy in Japan

Meiko Murayama

Introduction

The Covid-19 pandemic has had a significant impact worldwide on how we work. The pandemic has highlighted how digital technology is valuable and a barrier for those working in Japan. The year 2020 was a wake-up call for many organizations; the pace of change in digitization and digitalization accelerated. There is still skepticism regarding artificial intelligence (AI) technologies, though, and there has been a lack of necessary investment (Majima, 2017). When focusing on Japan, it has been renowned for its innovative technology, yet Japan lags in AI (Yamada et al., 2019). Masayoshi Son, the founder and the CEO of SoftBank, the world's biggest technology investor, warned his audience in a Tokyo tech conference just before the global pandemic that 'Japan is a developing country in AI' terms (Sano, 2019). This view is a widespread one (Kitoh, 2019; Kumar, 2019). The Japanese government published its first AI strategy in 2017 and admitted that its competitive position lagged in AI technology and has recently been allocating more resources to support education for AI and research and development. The IPA (Information-Technology Promotion Agency, Japan) published the *IT Human Resource White Paper* in August 2020, noting the increasing shortage of human resources in ICT (IPA, 2020). Furthermore, the 2020 *White Paper Information and Communication in Japan* was published by MIC (Ministry of Internal Affairs and Communication, 2020). The document also admitted that due to the pandemic, a wave of digitalization has reached into life and business activity that had not embraced it before, and digital technology has rapidly become essential.

This chapter sets out how a renewed purpose for business operations in the context of digital transformation (DX) does not merely involve maximizing shareholders' benefit but also achieving benefits for all stakeholders and embracing technological change. The chapter focuses on how Japan has been reforming its labor market and attempting to embrace digital technologies. A shortage of skilled human resources has hampered this strategy. Japan can provide insights and useful examples for the developed world as it struggles to shift toward DX and work toward 'Society 5.0.' The long-term impacts of Covid-19 are yet to become clear on national economies. However, it is more apparent now that it is essential to educate students and employees and prepare them for the 'post-Covid-19 world'; this critically requires us to embrace more sustainable and socially useful digital technologies.

Japan and Its Structural Problems

While many business organizations have been negatively affected by Covid-19, some technology giants' shares have soared, benefiting firms such as Google, Amazon, Facebook, and Apple (GAFA) (Paul and Rushe, 2020). It is worth noting that 50 years after Milton Friedman published an article where he claimed that 'the social responsibility of business is to increase its profit' (Meagher, 2020), this message appears now quite dissonant. One of the resulting impacts of his legacy can be seen in the GAFA technological giants' market dominance. This monopoly position can lead to abuses of power and a limitation on benefits to businesses and consumers. Covid-19 has accelerated pressure for business organizations to change for the better and ethically embrace digital technologies. Severe and varied impacts on companies and individuals during 2020, a significant series of inequalities have been highlighted.

The 'Business Roundtable,' consisting of CEOs of leading companies in the US, published a 'statement on a corporation's purpose in 2019. This moved away from the shareholder approach toward a stakeholder approach. The statement affirms the importance of valuing stakeholders such as employees, customers, and the local community. As part of the search for different approaches to business operations in this context, key phrases such as 'reset the clock,' 'Green recovery,' 'Sustainable recovery,' or 'Build Back Better (BBB)' have come to the fore during the pandemic (Kodaira, 2020). It is too early to analyze the impacts of the statement and the government's best intentions. However, greener, more ethical, and sustainable operations is a discernible direction of travel.

The prior context of the changes propelled by Covid-19 provided a challenging environment for Japan even before the pandemic. First, numerous factors affect the Japanese labor market adversely. The population has been declining, and the rate of shrinkage has been increasing. The population is expected to drop under 100 million in 2050 (from 128 million in 2008) (MIC, 2018; see Figure 2.1). Furthermore, 15–64 years old working-age group in 2017 was 75.96 million (60.0%) and it is expected to decrease to 59.78 million (53.9%) by 2040. Thus, the population structure has changed since 1997, with 28.1% of the total population over 65 years old – the highest in the world (Statistics Bureau of Japan, 2018).

These demographic trends have led to a falling working population. They will result in a shrinking domestic market, labor shortage, and disruption of the balance between the working people to cover pensions and

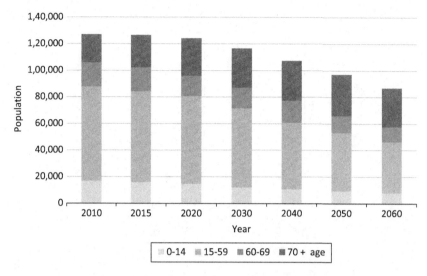

Figure 2.1 Future population of Japan.
Source: Cabinet office (2012).

social security systems. They may make Japan less attractive to foreign investment. The government identified Information Communication/ digital Technology (ICT) as possible salvation (MIC, 2018). The idea was that a decreasing working population should be tackled with increased productivity using digital technologies. New market developments should supplement the shrinking domestic demand through ICT, enhance opportunities abroad, and improve female and older generations to expand into the labor force. The increasing digitalization of businesses and associated ICT is set to play a critical role in the Japanese economy's future. The shortage of human resources in the ICT sector (there are two types: those who can *use* ICT skills and apply them in their jobs and those who can *develop* ICT/digital products and services) has been a significant issue. Figure 2.2 shows the gap between demand and supply for the number of ICT professionals predicted to 2030 (Mizuho Information and Research Institute, 2019), with three scenarios: low, medium, and high. The expected gap is between about 800,000 people and 160,000 people in those projections.

There are only two realistic options in the shorter term to narrow the gap. The first is to grow the ICT population; the most obvious way would be to increase the number of foreign ICT professionals working in Japan and raise productivity. Historically, Japan has not been open to immigration; however, various proactive measures have been implemented to increase foreign human resources in recent years. The government has been changing its approach on the supply side with regulation and law, enabling an increase of foreign workers in the country is passed. The

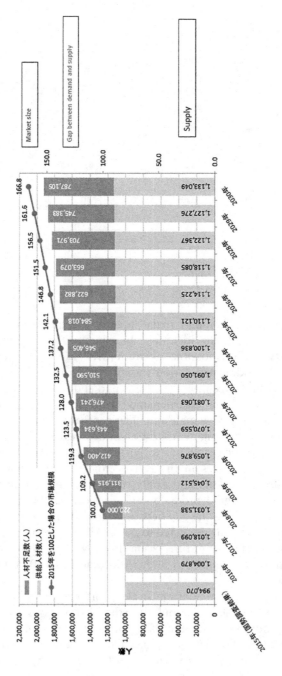

Figure 2.2 Japanese ICT human resource prediction to 2030 with higher ICT demand.
Source: Mizuho Information and Research Institute (2019).

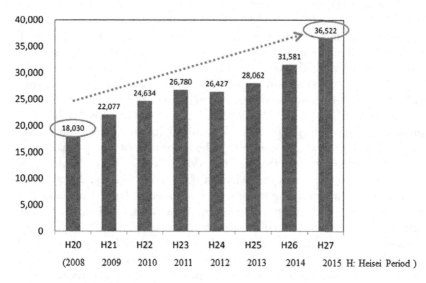

Figure 2.3 Increase of foreign workers in the ICT sector.
Source: METI (2018).

number of foreign workers in the ICT sector has been increasing (see Figure 2.3). The latest figures for foreign workers in the sector were 57,620 in 2018, and this number is expected to increase (MHLW, 2019a). These ICT workers are mainly from Japanese neighboring countries such as China and Hong Kong (47%), followed by South Korea (15%), Vietnam (6.3%), US (3.7%), Philippines (2.8%), Brazil (1.5%), UK (1.3%), and other countries (22.4%) (MHLW, 2019b).

Another indirect option is to increase the number of international students at Japanese universities and encourage them to work in the Japanese ICT sector after graduation. In 2019, over 312,000 international students increased from 299,000 in the previous year (MEXT, 2020). The number of international students at Japanese universities and colleges has been growing, despite a series of natural disasters in Japan. Another route is to promote young English teachers on the Government Japan Exchange and Teaching (JET) Program to remain in Japan (METI, 2015). There were over 5,700 such teachers in 2019. They are already familiar with Japanese culture and language – a significant advantage compared to attracting human resources directly from abroad. These are seen as an excellent potential recruitment pool. CLAIR (the organization that runs the JET program) has set up an internship scheme to gain different sets of skills and move into other sectors, including ICT (CLAIR, 2020a,b). Overall, recruiting foreign ICT human resources has been encouraged by the national government, and job fairs in Asian counties such as India,

China, and Singapore have been taking place with partnership effort from the public sector (METI, 2018; MHLW, 2020a).

The second method is to narrow the demand and supply gap in ICT human resources by increasing productivity. In 2018 Japanese productivity per hour ranked 21st among the 36 OECD member states. The productivity rate was at $46.80 in 2018 (this is around 60% of US productivity = $74.40) and productivity per person per year was $81,258 (about 60% of US = $132,127). There are many reasons for the low productivity levels in Japan. Atkinson (2020) attributes the main reason as the Japanese business structure, which consists of many small- and medium-sized enterprises (SMEs); the SME sector accounts for 99% of the total firms (The Small and Medium Enterprise Agency, 2019). Such SMEs cannot enjoy economies of scale compared to large firms, and this reduces productivity metrics. However, Shimazawa (2020) opposes the negative view stressing SMEs' value as essential parts of the Japanese economy – as they supply highly skilled products and services to large firms that they are unable to produce. Atkinson is right; however, in pointing out SMEs' disadvantaged position, they often lack resources to invest and struggle to provide sufficient ICT training (MEIT, MHLW, and MEXT, 2020). Morikawa (2018) emphasizes the importance of on-the-job and off-the-job training for those small- and medium-sized business organizations, as currently such corporate training is underinvested. Morikawa also criticizes government regulations and compliance needs as barriers to raising productivity. To increase productivity, Morikawa (2018) also noted the importance of raising the workforce's quality and formal education, stressing graduate education's role to enhance return on investment (ROI) and induce innovation. Indeed, the SME sector is now seeing some productivity increases as government actions take effect (MEIT, MHLW, and MEXT, 2020).

Japanese productivity has been low among OECD countries since 1970, and the recent figures are unsurprising (Japan Productivity Centre, 2019). Figure 2.4 shows the annual average growth of national ICT productivity of four countries, including Japan. The Japanese models are the lowest among the four highly advanced industrialized countries shown. However, if Japan can raise its rate to the same level as the German performance, then the shortage of ICT professionals will close (see Tables 2.1–2.3).

The Japanese have been known for long working hours, a rigid employment market and work styles, along with long commuting times, and paid holidays not being fully taken. There were many barriers for returning workers, including motherhood and underutilization of retired people. The government identified the decreasing and aging population as a barrier to economic growth, and work patterns had modernized to overcome this challenge. The Japanese government began a reform of work practices, including regulating long working hours, facilitating

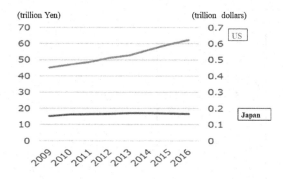

Figure 2.4 ICT investment of Japan and US.
Source: METI (2020).

Table 2.1 Growth of productivity in the ICT industry (year average)

Country	After 1995	2010s
US	5.4%	2.2%
Germany	4.2%	4.2%
France	3.1%	2.3%
Japan	2.4%	0.7%

Source: Mizuho Information Research Institute (2019).

Table 2.2 Balancing demand and supply of ICT human resources for growth in productivity

Scenario	Growth in IT demand	Growth in productivity	The gap between demand and supply (thousands)			
			2018	2020	2025	2030
1	1% (low)	1.84%	220	171	71	0
2	2–5% (med)	3.54%		230	103	0
3	3–9% (high)	5.23%		289	135	0

Source: Mizuho Information and Research Institute (2019).

more flexible ways of working, and ensuring paid holiday usage. This profound change has been called the 'Work Style Reform,' and April 2019 marked the introduction of the first laws of that reform agenda to limit extra working hours (for SMEs) and ensure employees took paid holidays (MHLW, 2020c). There are 11 action points in the reform, summarized into three main pillars:

Table 2.3   AI Robot scores for 2016 National Centre for University entrance examinations (mockup tests)

Subject	Japanese -200	Maths 1 (100)	Maths 2 (100)	English writing -200	English listening -50	Physics -100	Japanese history -100	World history -100	Total -960
National average %	96.8	54.4	46.5	92.9	26.3	45.8	47.3	44.8	437.8
AI robot %	96	70	59	95	14	62	52	77	525
AI robot Standard Dev.	49.7	57.8	55.5	50.5	36.2	59	52.9	66.3	57.1

Source: Arai and Ozaki (2016, p. 4).

- improvement in the practice of long *working hours*,
- ensuring *fair treatment* of workers, irrespective of their employment types, and
- introducing *diverse and flexible work styles*; and promote, enable, and enhance elderlies, women, the young generation, and foreign workers into the workforce (Council for the Realization of Work Style Reform, 2019).

A range of relevant reform laws is planned to follow, including considerable organizational reform as larger organizations have needed more time to prepare for the adjustments. The reform's overall aim is to 'realize the dynamic engagement of all citizens' (Cabinet Office, 2019). It is expected that the reforms will also lead to greater creativity and innovation (Giannetti and Madia, 2013; Hunter, 2019).

This broader reform agenda is a significant turning point for Japanese organizations and increasing numbers have been implementing teleworking. Teleworking has been one of the vital essential elements of flexible working during the pandemic, and the national government has set up a dedicated website to promote such work. MHLW (2020c) defines telework as tele-distance plus work and includes three types:

1 working from home,
2 mobile work – working while in transit using public transportation or in a café, and
3 working at a satellite office.

There have been various initiatives, funding, training, workshops, and exemplars awards (MHLW, 2020b). In Japan in 2012, 11.5% of businesses worked in this fashion, and it had risen to 20.2% in 2019 (MHLW 2020c). According to the OECD (2020), about 50% of the US and UK workers have been working from home by mid-April 2020, a much higher rate than Japan. However, Covid-19 and the national emergency pushed many organizations toward teleworking, and 34.5% of business organizations adopted it during the lockdown in 2020 (MHLW, 2020c). Google calculated a 22% reduction in the workforce is going to their offices during the national lockdown (Nikkei, 2020; NRI, 2020). Various factors determined the rate of teleworking adoption, such as organizations' size, sector, and type of jobs performed by employees (MHLW, 2020c). Almost two-thirds (65.3%) did not offer home working when asked in a July 2020 survey (MUFG, 2020). The top reasons for this were 'work not being able to be done via teleworking' (68.1%), 'concern of information security' (20.5%), 'lack of digitization of documents' (16.6%), 'lack of a system of managing employees' engagement and behavior' (14.6%), 'too costly to adopt ICT' (12.9%). These reasons reflect a slow adaptation of ICT (Kim, 2020; MUFG, 2020).

Digitized Society: Government Policies versus Industry Challenges

The DX involves a three-step process of (1) *digitization*, (2) *digitalization, and* (3) *digital transformation* (DX). However, many Japanese organizations are still struggling at the first digitization stage. The process is essential, as the OECD (2004) found a significant link between ICT adoption and economic performance.

The three terms above and associated DX stages are often used interchangeably. Yet, they differ: *digitization* is the stage of shifting from analog to digital forms (e.g., letters to email, documents to PDF). *Digitalization* involves using digital technology to change the business model or automate the process or operations, such as online library catalogs (Savic, 2019; Hassan, 2020). Then finally, DX is a more comprehensive organizational transformation process achieved through digitalization (Mergel et al., 2019). DX is a continuous and constant process of adjusting processes, services, and products as external needs change. Aoyama (2020) notes that DX requires organizational transformation to focus on customer satisfaction using AI, enabling competitive advantage. Senior management needs to be closely involved and take a decisive leadership role in the transformation to succeed with DX. However, Japan is behind in this global competitive shift compared to the US, China, and Germany. The reason for Japan being 'left behind' from this ICT revolution is explained before discussing policies and approaches for the future and the types of human resources needed for a DX nation.

The research found factors affecting ICT adaptation were features of organizations and epidemic effect (environment) were size, age, geographical location, workforce characteristics, R&D activities, subcontracting, exports propensity, a collaboration between firms, proximity to early adopters of ICT in the same industry and region (Giunta and Trivieri, 2007; Haller and Siedschlag, 2011). Fukao et al. (2016) found that size and age are critical factors for Japanese organizations. They found larger organizations have high ICT intensity. However, the age factor showed more complex results. Both very old and young firms tend to have higher ICT intensity.

Furthermore, small and young firms tend to have constraints in increasing ICT input, and smaller firms are less ICT intensive. The age of firms is another factor, and Japan has the largest concentration of longevity firms in the world (TDB, 2019). Older firms (more than 35 years old) contribute more than half of Japan's output (Inui and Kim, 2018). The senior management decision-makers are older, and some do not fully grasp the role and effects of ICT; they do not see the value in investing in it. Only 16% of the senior managers think it is essential compared to 75% of senior managers in the US, critical (Inui and Kim, 2018; Iwamoto, 2020). Japanese presidents' average age is also notable: 59.9 years old in 2019, a record high and partly reflects Japanese population structure (TDB, 2020) and traditional business seniority culture.

The competitive position of the Japanese manufacturing industry has decreased over the last few decades. The number of manufacturing firms fell by half, with one-third of the workforce shifted. The ratio of manufacturing GDP per entire industries has been steady and over 20%, labor productivity has been improved (Fujimoto, 2020a; METI, MXLW and MEXT, 2019; MEXT, 2010). As manufacturing is still the crucial foundation of the Japanese economy, to regain more substantial competitiveness among the US, China, EU, and rising Asian countries, Japan has to focus on its strengths and supplement its weaknesses. The US and China tend to have more resilience in manufacturing products using modular architecture (assemble standard parts), while Japan has a competitive advantage in integral architecture (Fujimoto, 2007). The latter requires a multi-skilled-labor-intensive approach, even in a digitalized society. The advance of digital technologies requires highly skilled jobs that cannot be done by machines. However, these enterprises also identified employees' needs to develop and apply ICT into their work (METI, MXLW and MEXT, 2020).

The global market share of Japanese end products has decreased. However, Japan still shows a strong presence in advanced materials such as ArF Photoresist parts, which has well over 80% market share in 2016 (METI, MXLW and MEXT, 2019). These products are essential in high-tech products such as automobiles, motorcycles, and precision machines. These highly functional materials and parts have kept a competitive advantage for Japanese manufacturing industries. Furthermore, recurrent natural disasters such as earthquakes, tsunami, and typhoons have made the sector and the supply chain more resilient against disasters, which has enabled them to recover quicker (Fujimoto, 2020b). During Covid-19, the reliability of Japanese factories' delivery dates made them more attractive while foreign competitors struggled to cope with the virus and associated uncertainties (Fujimoto, 2020b). The delivery expectations could continue to be a Japanese competitive advantage, so it is essential to educate the workforce to work in this sector with highly sophisticated craftsmanship with teamwork, plus ICT knowledge and skills (METI, MXLW and MEXT, 2020). Through successful DX cases, organizational ambidexterity to be necessary (see O'Reilly and Tushman, 2008; Aoyama, 2020), and dynamic capability is essential in surviving in such a changing environment (see Teece, 2014; Kikuzawa, 2018). Encouraging innovation and entrepreneurship have become even more critical.

Japan has undertaken some structural work reform to improve productivity and address digitization challenges; however, Inui and Kim (2018) found that after 2009, ICT investment in Japan was declining. ICT investment and productivity (i.e., total factor productivity – TFP) bear a significant relationship, and low investment has led Japan to be behind its competitors. While the US has enjoyed a considerable increase in TFP, Japan has slowed down in TFP growth after 1991 (Fukao et al., 2016). Inui and Kim's (2018) research concluded that low ICT investment in the past decade has led to low TFP in Japanese digitalization and DX, which has not been strong.

The more firms adopt innovative ICT, other firms in the same industry will follow (Al Bar and Hoque, 2019; Inui and Kim, 2018). Foreign ownership can also positively affect ICT investment behavior as more advanced management resources are imported and act to raise productivity. R&D and export propensity also have positive impacts on ICT investment. Japanese ICT investment has only increased 2.5 times (from 0.67 trillion yen to 1.67 trillion yen) from 1994 to 2016. In comparison, the US increased its investment six-fold in the same period (0.1025 trillion dollars to 0.623 trillion dollars) (METI, 2020). As shown in Figure 2.4, the Japanese ICT investment had stagnated between 2009 and 2016 and even slightly decreased from 2013 to 2016.

The process of attaining significant transformation toward ICT and AI technologies forms part of the 'super-smart society' concept and the 'Society 5.0' strategy, which was published in 2017 under the title 'Science Technology base plan 2017' which places technology, innovation, and science as a leading force for the new society (Cabinet Office, 2016). Society 5.0 develops from Society 1.0 ('hunter-gatherer'), Society 2.0 ('agricultural'), Society 3.0 ('industrialized'), and Society 4.0 ('information'). This fifth iteration of society is a sustainable, inclusive socio-economic system, powered by digital technologies such as big data analytics, AI, the Internet of Things, and robotics (Strategic Council for AI Technology, 2017; UNESCO, 2019). Society 5.0 is promoted to be sustainable and congruent with the UN's Sustainable Development Goals (SDGs). To support this, AI is regarded as an essential and core component, but there are barriers in Japan. First, critical data are not available (as well as the lack of ICT professionals). Unlike GAFA, Japanese organizations do not have the business model to collect big data for deep learning. Even where useful data are available, they are not always in a digital format or enabled for AI (Majima, 2017).

The technology strategy launched by the Japanese government in 2017 to address such barriers was complemented by the 'AI Strategy' in 2019 (Integrated Innovation Strategy Promotion Council Decision, 2019). The four objectives of the latter are:

1 Human resources – train the best AI human resources and attract AI human resources from abroad
2 Competitiveness – to become a global leader in the application of AI to strengthen industrial competitiveness
3 Establish and operate a technology system to achieve 'sustainability which embraces diversity'

4 Research and education – become a global leader in AI research, education, and social infrastructure network and accelerate AI R&D, human resources, and SDGs (Integrated Innovation Strategy Promotion Council Decision, 2019).

METI published the policy document 'Overcoming the digital cliff involving IT systems and full-fledged development of DX' between these policy documents (Study Group for Digital transformation, 2018). Together, these reflect the concern that if Japanese organizations do not undergo DX, the estimates are that the country's economy will lose up to 12 trillion yen (115 trillion dollars) after 2025 and continue to lose ground after that. Thus, urgent investment and change are needed, which cannot be left to the private and educational sectors alone.

It is worth noting that the *Keidanren* (Japan Business Federation), whose members consist of the largest Japanese public limited companies, with a strong voice in government, published a 'Digital Transformation: Opening the future through co-creation of values' document to support Society 5.0 (Keidanren, 2020). The most potent Japanese corporate leaders agree that Society 5.0 is critical to future success and can also help provide solutions for problems such as aging and the decreasing population. They also link DX as the single most significant factor to move toward Society 5.0 attributes.

Latterly the Japanese Prime Minister Suga, appointed in 2020, announced a National Digital Agency in 2021 to take charge of all things digital (Sekiguchi, 2020). Iwamoto (2020) is hopeful for the agency to take a leading role in developing and supporting standardized digital platforms for businesses to adopt. This will be a means to enable further innovation. The development and standardization of such platforms cannot be achieved by one firm. Thus, the role of the government is crucial.

Human Resources Development Challenges for Society 5.0

Life after Covid-19 seems uncertain, but Japanese society will not be the same. The Panasonic founder Konosuke Matsushita emphasized that the coming 'recession is a good chance for human resource development' (Kushida, 2020). This section focuses on human resources education and training needed in Japan's new era, focusing on ICT and based on the preceding sections' assessment.

Frey and Osborne (2013) shocked the world with their forecast of a potentially massive loss of employment due to computerization (automation). Yet, the role of a skilled employee is unlikely to be made redundant. Many other researchers followed Frey and Osborne (2013) and found that digital technologies, both substitute labor and acts, create new jobs (Autor, 2015; Iwamoto and Tagami, 2018). Arai and Higashinaka (2018) found both superiorities and limitations of AI by developing robots (algorithmic) to take national entrance examinations for Japanese universities. After five years of research and testing, the AI robots exceeded the average marks of human students (0.12 million students) in nearly all subjects (Arai and Ozaki, 2017; see Figure 2.5). After three years of the project, the AI robots' standard deviation for the test reached over 57 and positioned themselves in the top 25% of the whole students. The AI robots remembered all textbooks and Wikipedia, wrote a convincing essay, and scored good marks in multiple-choice questions. They have excelled as average students. The project team concluded that 'given the state of theory and near-future data and technologies, it is impossible to create an AI that can understand its interlocutor, accurately judge situations, and solve problems in cooperation with humans' (Arai and Ozaki, 2017, p. 5). Thus, it is stressed that AI depends on mathematical theories, including probability and statistics. Therefore, AI is incapable of the following four critical areas:

1 Non-standardized work in which input and output is not fixed
2 Type of work where no standardized judgment can be applied to decide correct answers
3 Draw the right judgments from minimal examples
4 Create innovation

This chapter's focus is to highlight the critical problem that the shortage of ICT human resources presents in Japan, given the context. The human resource shortage needs to be resolved if Japan successfully improves automation and achieves substantive DX. Educators must understand AI's capabilities and limitations and educate students on the necessary skills noted above so that AI and human input work together effectively and efficiently. MIC (2016) found that employers consider soft communication and coaching skills the most important, followed by problem-solving skills and language (reading, writing, and comprehension) skills. Application of ICT to many business operations areas, professional knowledge and skills, and digital knowledge and skills (such as mathematic, statistics, computer science) is essential in Society 5.0.

After Society 5.0 idea was published, the Japanese government has been proactive in supporting the ICT human resources. The budget for AI-related development has been raised from 14.7 billion yen to 38.95 billion yen for the 2020 fiscal year (SankeiBiz, 2020). The focus on education and training students to deal with data is now emphasized (such as providing one PC for one student at primary and junior high schools). An amount of 620 million yen (6 million dollars) was allocated for small- and medium-sized businesses to train employees to raise productivity, R&D, and human resource development in 2020. Resources are also assigned to educational institutions and in collaboration between industry and the educational sector (MEXT, 2019). IPA has facilitated a young ICT entrepreneurship program since 2000, and 1,700 young ICT engineers have been supported, and more than 255 entrepreneurs are running their own business through this scheme.

Universities, especially business schools, are important places for educating future and current employees and business leaders. As Japan will have an increasing female, semi-retired, and foreign workforce, their education and training needs will need renewed consideration. However, business schools have not adapted to a rapidly changing world and have been heavily criticized, especially in the realm of ethical education (Lau, 2010; Parker, 2018; Philips et al., 2016; Sigurjonsson et al., 2015). Business leaders after Covid-19 must be capable of navigating a rapidly changing world with globalization, sustainability, and ethics acting to steer decisions, not just focusing on short-term profit for shareholders. Ethics is included in the *AI strategy 2019* as a 'human-centered AI society principle' following OECD discussions on AI. Ethics has attracted research attention, and UNESCO and the G7 are currently setting an international framework on AI and ethics (Awad et al., 2018; Cabinet Office, 2019; Etzioni and Etzioni, 2017). Therefore, educators need to teach the skills required urgently by the industry (i.e., professional, ICT, and social skills) and train them to analyze business decisions to assess whether they are acting ethically and assisting with the UN SDGs. If this sounds wishful, then remember that AI learns based on decision-makers' actions, so if these decisions are based on mere 'profit maximization,' AI will reproduce outcomes in line with this direction.

As noted above, many business organizations in Japan have enjoyed longevity and continuity by applying fundamental principles to their business (Dooley and Ueno, 2020). Some traditional Japanese business enterprises originate from the Ohmi area in Japan and have inherited the moral code of the 'Sampo (three)-Yoshi' (good/satisfaction) approach, which has been passed down from the Edo period (Koshio and Nakajima, 2014; Sanpoyoshi, n.d.). Companies such as Itochu, Sumitomo, Toyota, Toray, Nishikawa, and Takashimaya department stores have some roots in the Ohmi tradition and follow this approach. This undertaking means the business must satisfy three dimensions: the 'seller,' the 'buyer,' and the 'society.' The Japanese style stakeholder approach to business may be one of the critical factors of longevity for these firms and guide the ethical business as we engage with AI and DX. We need to remember that ICT can enhance *Sampo-yoshi* and add value to society, not just enable cost cutting, increasing productivity, and profit maximization.

Covid-19 has changed people how to study/work. The change has brought opportunities and options and challenges (productivity, self-control, motivation, autonomy, communication, mental health, ICT skills). Business leaders know that on-the-job and off-the-job training is still essential (METI, MXLW and MEXT, 2020). Recurrent, continuous education, and training will be more critical as digital technology advances, and universities will need to provide extended programs to cater to this need. ICT education can start from primary school to inspire and raise awareness of the subjects and through to university and lifelong learning. Not only will it be academic institutions that offer such education and training, though, but industry themselves will also need to embrace this. ICT has also acted to widen options to study, too, as seen with massive open online courses and blended/e-learning. In a continually changing business environment, educating students and professionals should not just focus on only the 'what' but encourage 'why' (purpose or vision) questions. The following provides a framework/checklist of education and training/development. 'Why' learning comes first to prepare business organizations to create value for society, with sustainability an essential in the 2020s and beyond (Drucker, 1988; Kosio and Nakajima, 2014):

1 why – vision and purpose of the education/training
2 what – learning content, such as digital literacy, advanced IT skills, accounting, marking, communication skills, and ethics
3 who receives the education/training – early, broad approach
4 who is to deliver teaching/training – academics, industry professionals, cross-disciplinary
5 when teaching and learning takes place
6 where – place/location of education or training
7 how – in terms of methods of delivery
8 which – options to focus on

These influence each other, and agile training and education approaches are useful (see Sharp and Lang, 2018). For example, item #1, the 'why' has two elements; (a) primary purposes such as lean programming skills and (b) the goal – do the knowledge and skills acquired to contribute to the betterment of the society? The answers may not be straightforward; however, learners will need to analyze such a question if the ultimate vision or purpose of training and education to bring a more sustainable society – Society 5.0.

Conclusion

As noted, Japan has significant structural challenges of aging and decreasing population, which brings a series of economic problems, including shortages of critical human resources. The country once dominated with its manufacturing brands and enjoyed a reputation for technological achievement. However, the past is overshadowed by a receding economic power and slow transformation in the face of digital age demands and other humanitarian crises. Despite having a strong manufacturing sector, automation, adaptation of ICT, and AI have been very slow, while US Apple, Amazon, Facebook, Google and Microsoft, and Chinese Alibaba, Baidu, Tencent, and DiDi are making a large profit through new digital technologies. The Japanese government has changed its course and is now taking an aggressive growth strategy to support digitization and digitalization to achieve Society 5.0.

Fujimoto (2020b) suggests the economy after Covid-19 depends on sustainability, digital, and globalization ('SDG'). The shock of Covid-19 has accelerated the digital agenda which the country desperately needs. Digitization and digitalization are required to achieve DX, making the Japanese organizations globally more competitive. It is still not clear what the future would be after Covid-19. However, the Japanese economy is set to yet come together around the manufacturing sector. Slow digitization and digitalization and AI implementation will be a threat. However, various government regulatory changes, investment, and support will facilitate SMEs' automation and increase ICT/AI human resources. Work Style Reform's aims also are geared to increase productivity and the working population's quantum, but the impacts are yet to be seen. The future is not certain, but one thing is sure – that Japan is building a future based on its traditional strengths, and digital technologies are to be applied to support productivity in those sectors. Digital technology will be essential to solving many of Japan's challenges, but they are just tools. Ironically the key to the DX and Society 5.0 lies in people: investment in skills, education, and human capital that can drive DX is critical for Japan post-Covid and most likely worldwide. The aspiration in Japan is that they will also aid broader and long-term global challenges.

References

AlBar, A. M. and Hoque, M. R. (2019) Factors affecting the adoption of information and communication technology in small and medium enterprises: a perspective from rural Saudi Arabia. *Information Technology for Development*, 25(4), pp. 715–738, DOI: 10.1080/02681102.2017.1390437.

Aoyama, M. (2020) *DX and its promotion strategy*. 17 November. [webinar], Tokyo, JBPress DX world, Located: https://jbpress-expo.smktg.jp/public/application/add/108#online-seminar.

Arai, N. and Ozaki, K. (2016) *Cultivating human resources for the era of digitalization*. NIRA (Nippon Institute for Research Advancement) Opinion Paper 31. Available from: www.nira.or.jp/pdf/e_opinion31.pdf

Arai, N. and Ozaki, K. (2017) *Cultivating human resources for the era of digitalization*. NIRA (Nippon Institute for Research Advancement) Opinion Paper 31. Available from: www.nira.or.jp/pdf/e_opinion31.pdf.

Arai, N. and Higashinaka, R. (2018) *Artificial intelligence project 'can robot enter Tokyo University?' Achievements and limitations of the third AI boom.* Tokyo: Tokyo University Press.

24 *Meiko Murayama*

Atkinson, D. (2020) The main reason for low productivity in Japan is owing to small to medium size businesses. *ToyoKeizai*. 27 March, Available from: https://toyokeizai.net/articles/print/339534?ismmark=a.

Autor, D. H. (2015) Why are there still so many jobs? The history and future of workplace automation. *Journal of Economic Perspectives*, 29(3), pp. 3–30. Available from: https://economics.mit.edu/files/11563.

Awad, E., Dsouza, S., Kim, R., Schulz, J., Henrich, J. Shariff, A., Bonnefon, J-F. and Rahwan, I. (2018) The moral machine. *Nature*, November, 563, pp. 59–78. Available from: https://doi.org/10.1038/s41586-018-0637-6.

Cabinet Office (2016) *The 5th Science and Technology Basic Plan*. Available from: www8.cao.go.jp/cstp/kihonkeikaku/index5.html.

Cabinet Office (2019) *Small and medium size business are to face 'Work Style Reform.'* Available from www.gov-online.go.jp/cam/hatarakikata/.

CLAIR (The Council of Local Authority for International Relations) (2020a) *JET carrier up internship program*. Available from: http://jetprogramme.org/ja/jetinternship/>.

CLAIR (2020b) *Jet leaflet* http://jetprogramme.org/ja/nin-pamphlet/

Council for the Realization of Work Style Reform (2019) *The Japan's plan for dynamic engagement of all citizens*. Available from: https://japan.kantei.go.jp/content/jpnplnde_en.pdf.

Dooley, B. and Ueno, H. (2020) This Japanese shop is 1,020 years old. It know a bit about surviving crises. *New York Times*, 2 December. Available from: www.nytimes.com/2020/12/02/business/japan-old-companies.html?action=click&module=Editors%20Picks&pgtype=Homepage.

Drucker, P. (1988) *Management*. London: Heinemann.

Etzioni, A. and Etzioni, O. (2017) Incorporating ethics into artificial intelligence. *Journal of Ethics*, 21, pp. 403–418. DOI 10.1007/s10892-017-9252-2.

Frey, C. B. and Osborne, M. A. (2013) *The future of employment: how susceptible are jobs to computerisation?* Available from: www.oxfordmartin.ox.ac.uk/downloads/academic/The_Future_of_Employment.pdf.

Fujimoto, T. (2007) Architecture-based comparative advantage — a design information view of manufacturing. *Evolutionary Institutional Economic Review*, 4, pp. 55–112. Available from: https://doi.org/10.14441/eier.4.55.

Fujimoto, T. (2020a) Monozukuri-Japan conference: how can Japan win in the world in manufacturing industry? 13 January, *Nikkan Kogyo Sinbun*. Available from: www.nikkan.co.jp/articles/view/00544884.

Fujimoto, T. (2020b) Infectious dieses & manufacturing in digitalization period. [webinar] 19 November. JBPress DX world, Tokyo. Available from: https://jbpress-expo.smktg.jp/public/application/add/108#online-seminar.

Fukao, K., Ikeuchi, K., Kim, Y. and Kwon, H. (2016) *Why was Japan left behind in the ICT revolution?* RIETI (Research Institute of Economy, Trade and Investing) Discussion Paper Series, 15-E-043. Available from: www.rieti.go.jp/jp/publications/dp/15e043.pdf.

Giannetti, C. and Madia, M. (2013) Work arrangements and firm innovation: is there any relationship? *Cambridge Journal of Economics*, 37, pp. 273–297 doi:10.1093/cje/bes067.

Giunta, A. and Trivieri, F. (2007) Understanding the determinants of information technology adoption: evidence from Italian manufacturing firms. *Applied Economics*, 39(10), pp. 1325–1334, DOI: 10.1080/00036840600567678.

Haller, S. A. and Siedschlag, J. (2011) Determinants of ICT adoption: evidence from firm-level data. *Applied Economics*, 43(26), pp. 3775–3788, DOI: 10.1080/00036841003724411.

Hasan, K. (2020) Undergoing successful digital transformations: to properly navigate the course, it is vital to understand the difference between digitisation, digitalization and digital transformation. *The Business Times Singapore*, 2 July. Available from: https://search.proquest.com/docview/2419340869?accountid=13460&pq-origsite=summon.

Hunter, P. (2019) *Remote working in research: an increasing usage of flexible work arrangements can improve productivity and creativity.* EMBO reports 20.1 DOI 10.15252/embr.201847435.

Integrated Innovation Strategy Promotion Council Decision (2019) *AI Strategy 2019.* Available from: www.kantei.go.jp/jp/singi/ai_senryaku/pdf/aistratagy2019en.pdf.

Inui, T. and Kim, Y. (2018) *Why Japanese firms were slow in adopting IT.* RIET Discussion paper 18-J014. Available from: www.rieti.go.jp/jp/publications/summary/18040005.html.

IPA (Information-Technology Promotion Agency, Japan) (2020) *IT Human Resource White Paper.* Available from: www.ipa.go.jp/jinzai/jigyou/about.html.

Iwamoto, K (2020) *Why Japan is far behind in digital in the world.* RIETI. Available from: www.rieti.go.jp/jp/columns/s20_0012.html.

Iwamoto, K. and Tagami, Y. (2018) *Digitization, computerization, networking, automation, and the future of jobs in Japan.* RIETI Policy Discussion Paper Series 18-P-013. Available from: www.rieti.go.jp/jp/publications/pdp/18p013.pdf.

Japan Productive Center (2019) *International comparison of labor productivity.* Available from: www.jpc-net.jp/research/list/comparison.html.

Keidanren (2020) *Digital transformation – opening up the future through co-creation of values* (summary). 19 May. Available from: www.keidanren.or.jp/en/policy/2020/038_summary.pdf.

Kikuzawa, K. (2018) The reason why Kodak fail and Fujifilm survived. *President online.* 3 December 2018. Available from: https://president.jp/articles/-/27318.

Kim, M. (2020) *Factors of reasons why teleworking has not widely implemented in Japanese organisations.* 13 July. NLI Research Institute. Available from: www.nli-research.co.jp/report/detail/id=64927?site=nli.

Kitoh, Y. (2019) Japanese companies slow in adopting AI-seniority being problem. *ITMedia.* 20 November. Available from www.itmedia.co.jp/business/articles/1911/20/news051.html.

Kodaira, R. (2020) Green leads "better recovery" after corona virus. *Nihon Keizai Shinbun.* Available from: www.nikkei.com/article/DGXMZO62028640Z20C20A7I10000/.

Koshio, A. and Nakajima, M. (2014) 'Sanpoyoshi': business model – essential factor for eternal continuity. Project Design Online. *The Graduate School of Project Design.* October. Available from: https://www.projectdesign.jp/201410/designforpd/001666.php.

Kumar, V. (2019) Japan losing its tech position as it lags in adopting artificial intelligence. *Analytics insight.* Available from: www.analyticsinsight.net/japan-losing-tech-position-lags-adopting-artificial-intelligence/.

Kushida, K. (2020) *The true value of developing 'AI human resources' lies in problem setting abilities*. NIRA opinion paper. *No. 51*. July. Available from: www.nira.or.jp/pdf/opinion51.pdf.

Lau, C. L. L. (2010) A step forward: ethics education matters! *Journal of Business Ethics*, 92, pp. 565–584. DOI 10.1007/s10551-009-0173-2.

Majima, K. (2017) Japan as 'AI developing country': Who are responsible for this – government or business organisations or attitudes of Japanese? JBPress. 9 November. Available from: https://jbpress.ismedia.jp/articles/-/51573?page=1.

Meagher, M. (2020) Fifty years of shareholder value have swollen monopoly power. *Financial Times*. Available from: www-ft-com.eur.idm.oclc.org/content/de8b9a1c-df69-44e5-b571-81f4651de050.

Mergel, I., Edelman, N. and Haug, N. (2019) Defining digital transformation: results from expert interviews. *Government Information Quarterly*, 36(4). Available from: https://doi.org/10.1016/j.giq.2019.06.002.

METI (Ministry of Economy, Trade and Industry) (2015) *On utilization of foreign IT human resources*. Available from: www.meti.go.jp/shingikai/sankoshin/shomu_ryutsu/joho_keizai/it_jinzai/pdf/002_05_01.pdf.

METI (2018) Expanding foreign IT human resources. *METI Journal Policy* Features/Globalisation within. Vol. 5. 16 February. Available from: https://meti-journal.jp/p/195/.

METI (2020) *Committee for creating sustainable corporate value through realising dialogue*. Reference material no. 4 11 June. Available from: www.meti.go.jp/shingikai/economy/sustainable_kigyo/pdf/006_04_00.pdf.

MEITI, MXLW and MEXT (2019) *White Paper on Monodzukuri 2019*. Available from: www.meti.go.jp/report/whitepaper/mono/2019/index.html.

MEITI, MXLW & MEXT (2020) *White Paper on Monodzukuri 2020*. Available from: www.meti.go.jp/report/whitepaper/mono/2020/index.html.

MEXT (Ministry of Education, Culture, Sport, Science and Technology) (2010) *Reference material 3*. Available from: www.mext.go.jp/b_menu/shingi/chukyo/chukyo10/shiryo/__icsFiles/afieldfile/2010/12/15/1299347_3.pdf.

MEXT (2019) *AI human resource development through collaboration between industry and academic sectors by MEXT*. Reference material no. 4. Available from: www.mext.go.jp/component/a_menu/education/detail/__icsFiles/afieldfile/2019/01/30/1413186_4_1.pdf.

MEXT (2020) *Research on 'foreign students enrolment' and 'Japanese studying abroad'*. Press release. Available from: www.mext.go.jp/content/20200421-mxt_gakushi02-100001342_1.pdf.

MHLW (Ministry of Health, Labour and Welfare) (2019a) *Summary of employment of foreign workers deriving through notification by business owners*. Available from: www.mhlw.go.jp/stf/newpage_03337.html.

MHLW (2019b) *Tables of employment of foreign workers deriving from notification by business owners*. Available from: www.mhlw.go.jp/content/11655000/000472893.pdf.

MHLW (2020a) *Handbook of employing and retention of foreign IT human resources*. Available from: www.mhlw.go.jp/content/11600000/000617377.pdf.

MHLW (2020b) *Teleworking general portal site*. Available from: https://telework.mhlw.go.jp/telework/.

MHLW (2020c) *Reference material 'current situation of teleworking'. Committee of future workstyle with teleworking.* 17 August. Available from: www.mhlw. go.jp/content/11911500/000662173.pdf.

MIC (Ministry of Internal Affairs and Communication) (2016) *White Paper Information and Communication in Japan.* Available from: www.soumu. go.jp/johotsusintokei/whitepaper/h28.html.

MIC (2018) *White Paper Information and Communication in Japan.* Available from: www.soumu.go.jp/johotsusintokei/whitepaper/ja/h30/html/nd101100. html.

MIC (2020) *White Paper Information and Communication in Japan.* Available from: www.soumu.go.jp/johotsusintokei/whitepaper/.

Mizuho Information and Research Institute, Inc. (2019) *Research Report on Supply and Demand of Japanese IT Workforce.* Research report for METI. Available from: www.meti.go.jp/policy/it_policy/jinzai/houkokusyo.pdf.

Morikawa, M. (2018) *Productivity: misunderstanding and truth.* RITEI 29 November, BBL Seminar. Available from: www.rieti.go.jp/jp/events/bbl/ 18112901_morikawa.pdf.

MUFG (Mitsubishi UFJ Research & Consulting) (2020) *Research on teleworking and human resource management.* MHLW 'Committee of future telework workstyle' Reference material 16 November. Available from: www.mhlw. go.jp/content/11911500/000694957.pdf.

Nikkei (2020) According to a survey conducted by a private sector, rate of teleworking has decreased. *Nikkei Shinbun* 11 June. Available from: www. nikkei.com/article/DGXMZO60232970R10C20A6TJ2000.

NRI (Nomura Research Institute) (2020) *Shirking remote working: Do not give up due to the experience during the national lock down. Summary* 13 July. Available from: www.nri.com/jp/keyword/proposal/20200713.

OECD (2004) *Economic impact of ICT: measurement, evidence and implications.* Available from: www.oecd-ilibrary.org/docserver/9789264026780-en.pdf?ex pires=1608556707&id=id&accname=guest&checksum=6D798B1F4CEC14 333BD4A336142C8EB3.

OECD (2020) *OECD employment outlook 2020: worker security and the Covid-19 crisis.* Available from: www.oecd-ilibrary.org/sites/1686c758-en/1/ 3/1/index.html?itemId=/content/publication/1686c758-en&_csp_=fc80786ea 6a3a7b4628d3f05b1e2e5d7&itemIGO=oecd&itemContentType=book#sect ion-d1e3069.

O'Reilly, C. A. and Tushman, M. L. (2008) Organizational ambidexterity: past, present and future. *Academy of Management Perspectives,* 27(4), pp. 324–338 Available from: www.jstor.org/stable/43822033.

Parker, M. (2018) Why we should bulldoze the business school. *The Guardian.* 27 April. Available from: www.theguardian.com/news/2018/apr/27/ bulldoze-the-business-school.

Paul, K. and Rushe, D. (2020) Tech giants' share soar as companies benefit from Covid-19 pandemic. *The Guardian.* Available from: www.theguardian.com/ business/2020/jul/30/amazon-apple-facebook-google-profits-earnings.

Philips, F., Hsieh, C. H. Ingene, C. and Golden, L. (2016) Business schools in crisis. *Journal of Open Innovation: Technology, Market, and Complexly.* pp. 1–10. DOI 10.1186/s40852-016-0037-9.

SankeiBiz (2020) Government. 390 billion yen for AI related budget, facilitate growth with national strategy. *SankeiBiz.* Available from: www.sankeibiz.jp/macro/news/200203/mca2002030746006-n1.htm?.

Sano, M. (2019) Son, CEO of Softbank warns 'Japan is developing country of AI' with sense of crisis. Any chance to catch up? *Nikkei X Trend.* Available from: https://xtrend.nikkei.com/atcl/contents/technology/00005/00027/.

Sanpoyoshi (n.d.) Ohmi merchant family precepts: *Sanpoyoshi.* Available from: https://sanpo-yoshi.net/download/.

Savic, D. (2019) From digitization, through digitalization, to digital transformation. *Online searchers.* 43(1). Information Today inc. Available from: https://go.gale.com/ps/i.do?p=ITOF&u=rdg&id=GALE%7CA569457603&v=2.1&it=r&sid=summon%2Chttps%3A%2F%2Fgaleapps.gale.com%2Fapps%2Fauth.

Sekiguchi, W. (2020) A digital agency would crown Japan's IT strategy. *The Japan Times.* 16 October. Available from: www.japantimes.co.jp/opinion/2020/10/16/commentary/japan-commentary/digital-agency-crown-japans-strategy/.

Sharp, J. H. and Lang, G. (2018) Agile in teaching and learning: conceptual framework and research agenda. *Journal of Information Systems Education.* 29(2), pp. 45–52. Available from: https://jise.org/volume29/n2/JISEv29n2p45.pdf.

Shimazawa, S. (2020) Opposing Atkinson – Japanese low productivity attributes to large corporations. *Yahoo Japan News.* 21 October. Available from: https://news.yahoo.co.jp/byline/shimasawamanabu/20201021-00203988/.

Sigurjonsson, T., Arnardottir, A., Vaiman, V. and Rikhardsson, P. (2015) Managers' views on ethics education in business schools: aneEmpirical study. *Journal of Business Ethics,* 130(1), pp. 1–13. 18 December 2020. Available from: www.jstor.org/stable/24703066.

Statistics Bureau of Japan (2018) *International comparison of senior citizens.* Available from: www.stat.go.jp/data/topics/topi1135.html.

Strategic Council for AI Technology (2017) *Artificial intelligence technology strategy.* 31 March. Available from: www.nedo.go.jp/content/100865202.pdf.

Study Group for Digital transformation (2018) Overcoming the digital cliff involving IT systems and full-fledged development of DX, METI. Available from: www.meti.go.jp/shingikai/mono_info_service/digital_transformation/20180907_report.html.

TDB (Teikokku Data Banks) (2019) Longevity firms with over century operation – more than 33,000. *Special report.* 8 January. TDB. Available from: www.tdb.co.jp/report/watching/press/pdf/p190101.pdf.

TDB (2020) Average age of presidents – 59.9 years old: continuous increase and new record again. *Special report.* 28 January. Available from: www.tdb.co.jp/report/watching/press/pdf/p200108.pdf.

Teece, D. (2014). The foundations of enterprise performance: dynamic and ordinary capabilities in an (economic) theory of firms. *Academy of Management Perspectives,* 28(4), pp. 328–352. Available from: www.jstor.org/stable/43822373.

The Small and Medium Enterprise Agency (2019) *White Paper on small and medium enterprise in Japan.* Available from: www.chusho.meti.go.jp/pamflet/hakusyo/2019/PDF/chusho/00Hakusyo_zentai.pdf.

UNESCO (2019) *Japan pushing ahead with Society 5.0 to overcome chronic social challenges. UNESCO science report: towards 2030.* 21 February. Available from: https://en.unesco.org/news/japan-pushing-ahead-society-50-overcome-chronic-social-challenges.

Yamada, C., Takemura, R., Fukushima, T. and Ouchi, N. (2019) Investigating problems of research and development of artificial intelligence technology in Japan. *IEEE International Conference on Industrial Engineering and Engineering Management (IEEM).* DOI: 10.1109/IEEM44572.2019.8978618.

3 Futurology Reorientation Nexus
Fourth Industrial Revolution

Brighton Nyagadza

> The fourth industrial revolution will have a monumental impact on the global economy, so vast and multifaceted that it makes it hard to disentangle one particular effect from the next.
> (Klaus Schwab, 2016. The Fourth Industrial Revolution)

Introduction

Fourth Industrial Revolution (4IR) has the potential to transform the International Management Education (IME) futurology both positively and negatively. It has brought serious prompts to the educators to develop dynamic curricula, bridging the gap between physical, digital, and biological setups as seen well before the advent. It has brought the development of comprehensive disruptive technologies. The 4IR has arrived with disruptive technologies such as artificial intelligence (AI), blockchain, big data, Internet of Things (IoT), 3D bio-printing and quantum computing, extended reality (augmented reality, virtual reality, mixed reality), and platform businesses. The technologies directly impact how IME shall be delivered to students across the globe. This automation has been increased (McAfee and Brynjolfsson, 2017; Kim, 2020) with the education systems and methodologies. To support these emerging technologies, scholars have explored the adaptation of the IoT and educational platforms for IME activities (Amodu et al., 2019; Dozier, Shen, Sweetser, and Barker, 2016; Scott, 2010; Tankosic et al., 2016; Wang, 2015). Other scholars have described the new development with terms such as digital, online, or electronic learning (Amodu et al., 2019; Petrovici, 2014; Philips and Young, 2009; Vercic et al., 2015).

Currently, many of the decisions that humans make (the educators) shall be made by the digital algorithms, which are much sharper inaccuracy, provided there is no unbiased data, which may be erroneous (Manyika, 2013; McAfee and Brynjolfsson, 2017; Kim, 2020). Digitally connected educational technologies with intelligent systems can revolutionize and optimize digital educational platforms with the interconnection of network systems, thus IoT (Younus et al., 2009; Bauernhansl et al., 2014; Heyman et al., 2014; Micheler et al., 2019; Nyagadza, 2020).

Challenges of the 4IR emerging technologies in the delivery of the IME include, but not limited to, sufficiency issues related to maturity befitting technological disruption and affordability (Ordoobadi, 2011; Van Der Velden et al., 2012; Micheler et al., 2019) for interoperability reasons (Danila et al., 2016; Micheler et al., 2019). The issues depict the importance of IME digital technologies befitting professional students' needs across the globe. However, complexities are still visible on how the access to and control over the digital educational resources has yielded the expected benefits. Eliminating human interaction in education can be difficult as emotions and feelings are necessary for the IME educators and the students in their entirety. The following section looks deeply at the 4IR, in detail succeeded by a section on current IME.

Fourth Industrial Revolution (4IR) Context

Schwab (2016) proposed that 4IR is premised on integrating technologies that blur the lines between the physical, digital, and biological spheres and disrupt the industries of all countries. As it is, 4IR has an agile growth from the development of the steam engine in the 18th century to the construction of massive and efficient speedy bullet trains. The revolution has brought social changes to the extent that people are becoming more and more urbanized in settling in their societies. There was further development of automation, which shows the emergence of digital technology, computers, and electronics beginning of the 1950s. 4IR follows the digital revolution's footsteps, but it is different from it (Schwab, 2016; WEF, 2018; AfDB, 2019). Due to this, industries are developing new ways of dealing with disruption affected by the current status quo within the strategic value chains and operations (Table 3.1).

Table 3.1 Main characteristics of industrial revolutions

Period	Transition period	Energy resource	Main technical achievement	Main developed industries	Transport means
I: 1760–1900	1860–1900	Coal	Steam engine	Textile, steel	Train
II: 1900–1960	1940–1960	Oil, electricity	Internal combustion engine	Metallurgy, auto, machine building	Train, car
III: 1960–2000	1980–2000	Nuclear energy, natural gas	Computers, robots	Auto, chemistry	Car, plane
IV: 2000-	2000–2010	Green energies	Internet, 3D printer, genetic engineering	High-tech industries	Electric car, ultra-fast train

Source: Prisecaru, P. (2016). "Challenges of the Fourth Industrial Revolution". *Knowledge Horizons. Economics*, 8(1), 57–62.

There is sufficient evidence to argue that the current disruptive transformations are not a mere extension of the Third Revolution but marks the 4IR's arrival as a unique phase in terms of scope, velocity, and systems impact on International Management (IME). With exponential rather than linear pace, the 4IR is disrupting almost every industry in every country (Xu et al., 2018; Nyagadza et al., 2020a). As the forces of technology increase, there is a mega shift in the IME institutions operations, leading to the reexamination of the way they keep and guard their professional educational resources sustainably (Schwab, 2016; World Bank, 2018; Nyagadza et al., 2020c).

Global educational institutions and ministerial governments need to incubate agile ideas for their citizens and public authorities to yield sustainable human capital development and profitability. There are potential benefits that result from the development of the 4IR due to the changes that the technology fosters, ranging from, but not limited to, economic, social, and environmental benefits. The following are descriptors of critical 4IR emerging technologies and their meaning as applied in different fields of study (Table 3.2).

International Management Education Changes

The current IME changes require a complete revolution of the curriculum constructs, which is meant to incubate rethinking on the knowledge tenets and highly emancipating pedagogy in line with the digital age that is eventually unrolling. Through the use of digital educational media, many IME professionals are learning in their homes' comfort. The television sets, radio transmission, either online or conventionally, can access as they do it. A comfortable and profitable way to reach the targeted audience (students) is the use of digital (educational) media platforms (Morely, 2016). The digital IMEs have revitalized their identities, ethos, aims, and values, creating a sense of individuality and differentiating their branding (van Riel and Balmer 1997; Kapferer 1997; de Chernatony, 1999; Harrison Price and Bell, 1998; Harris and de Chernatony, 2001; Nyagadza, 2020; Nyagadza et al., 2020b). The concept of corporate image, reputation, branding, and identity has been discussed highly by scholars in various disciplines, including IME (Caruana, 1997; Balmer, 2001; Harris and de Chernatony, 2001; Helms, 2007; Knox and Bickerton, 2003; Hatch and Schultz 2003; Balmer and Gray 2003; Kay, 2006; Balmer and Greyser, 2006; Eberl and Schwaiger, 2005; Wartick, 1992, 2002; Fombrun, 1998; Spotts and Weinberger, 2010; Nyagadza, 2020) inclusive of IME.

Critical IME Professional Reorientation during 4IR

There are some changes to the management science, pure sciences, data sciences, and technology curriculum expanding students' capacity to deal

Table 3.2 Descriptors of key Fourth Industrial Revolution (4IR) emerging technologies meanings interweaved to International Management (IME)

Emerging Technology	Description
Artificial Intelligence (AI)	System recognizing complex patterns, processing information, drawing conclusions and making decisions. System which may evolve in the future and which would be truly autonomous in its reasoning and thinking and be able to improve itself entirely independently from humans.
Big Data analytics	Complex process of examining large and varied data sets (Big Data) to uncover information including hidden patterns, unknown correlations, market trends, customer preferences, and other relevant insights that can help organizations make informed decisions.
Blockchain	Delivery of computing services (servers, storage, databases, networking, software, analytics, and intelligence) over the internet ('the cloud')
Fifth-generation wireless (5G)	Latest iteration of cellular technology engineered to greatly increase the speed and responsiveness of wireless networks.
The Internet of things (IoT)	System of interrelated computing devices, mechanical and digital machines, objects, animals or people that are provided with unique identifiers (UIDs), and the ability to transfer data over a network without requiring human-to-human or human-to-computer interaction.
Autonomous vehicle	Driverless vehicle that can move and guide itself without human input.
Drone	Unmanned flying vehicle that is controlled remotely
Additive manufacturing	Process of producing products by computer-aided, layer-by-layer addition of material(s), application of this 3D printing technology on an industrial scale.
Quantum computing technologies	Quantum computers leverage quantum mechanical phenomena to manipulate information, relying on quantum bits, or qubits
Virtual reality (VR)	VR: artificial, computer-generated simulation, or recreation of a real-life environment or situation.
Augmented reality (AR)	AR: technology that layers computer-generated enhancements on top of an existing reality in order to make it more meaningful through the ability to interact with it.
Robotics	Industry related to the engineering, construction, and operation of robots (machine designed to execute one or more tasks automatically with speed and precision).

Source: African Development Bank (AfDB) (2019).

with complex situations. IME academics have to respond as quickly as possible as the 4IR technologies' influence on educational practice is still yet unknown. However, the certainty is that change will be triggered soon. In the 4IR, the management students. These significant concerns are more not to be integrated from technological advancement, and the 4IR will have to reduce the categorizations between humanities and STEM programs.

The IME should explore newly emerging conceptions of self and identity, including discourses related to social relations, freedom, and generic versus social determinism. Globalization will increase how IME curriculum changes would lead to rapid identity, societal, and national obligations. The speed of the change may cause complexities and volatility in the system of teaching and learning effectiveness. Academics and professionals must note that the rapidity of responses to changes caused by 4IR to IME can help recognize students' training and manage proliferation and building interconnected pedagogical systems (Rojewski and Hill, 2017; Nyagadza et al., 2020a). The changes to the management education system will assist the students in upskilling them as soon as they finish their study programs.

In the IME curriculum, there is a need to educate and reeducate the students to develop and shape the current high, rapidly dynamic 4IR emerging technologies (Penprase, 2018). The reeducation will make the professionals, academics, and students align them with scientific and technological advancements. Implications to them would be continued renewal and update of their skills, as per contemporary discoveries and creative development forms.

Theoretical Framework

The theoretical framework that grounds this work are the technology acceptance model (TAM) and innovation diffusion theory (IDT), anchoring this chapter. The TAM was initiated by Fred Davis in 1986 and has gone through a series of validations and modifications (Nyagadza, 2019a). The purpose of the theory is to describe factors that govern technology acceptance, information technology, behavioral usage, and give a prudent theoretical explanatory model (Bourchard, 2010; Nyagadza, 2019a). This theory links IME with the 4IR. The model is an extension of the theory of reasoned action by Ajzen and Fishbein (Kumar, 2013; Nyagadza, 2019a). Ducey (2013) posited that the TAM variables are perceived ease of use and perceived usefulness; these are critical success factors on technology acceptance and user behavior. Teo et al. (2011) observed that several factors promote the use and acceptance of technology, especially in situations where professional management students work in line with changes taking place in the academic circles. The individual differences, beliefs, attitudes, social influences, and situational influences as determinants foster the interaction of technology usage and the promotion of the acceptance or rejection of technology (Teo 2010). They also postulate that individual behavior is influenced by an intention to accept or reject technology usage. Therefore, using technology is because of accepting or rejecting technology (Nyagadza, 2019b). The orientation leads to the evaluation of the next theory, IDT.

The IDT has five characteristics: relative advantage, compatibility, complexity, trial-ability, and observability. The innovative variables look very different from others; however, they have a lot to do with each other in information systems. Moore (1991) showed that the potential use and relative advantage denote the same thing while capturing the complexity of the IDT, as much as the variables sound different. The adopters often have different perceptions of the IDT characteristics compared to non-adopters (Kotler, 2010). This same applies to the IME, academics, and students in line with the changes brought about by the 4IR.

The characteristics of innovation affect the adoption rate (Keller, 2003). Some educational services and products are readily accepted, while others take some time to be adopted (Keller, 2003; Nyagadza, 2019a). If innovation could be of relative advantage, better than the existing system, comparably consistent with the needs of consumers as well as with a decent measure of complexity, easier to use and understand, which will most likely be favorable to the stakeholders and quickly adopted (Ching and Ellis, 2004). Lee (2015) supported this by arguing that the perceived relative advantage, complexity, and compatibility of innovations play an essential role in adopting agent banking. Nyagadza (2019a) discussed the IDT by Rogers (1993) with attributes, namely complexity, compatibility, relative advantage, and trialability, and found that comparative advantage, compatibility, and perceived ease of use to be significantly related to the attitude to use of disruptive technologies.

4IR digital disruptive technologies include the use of smart mobile devices, social media networks, websites, email platforms, digital learning, etc. (Brown and Duguid, 1994; Bower and Christensen, 1995; Kurzweil, 2005; Tripsas, 2009; Anderson et al. 2011; Utesheva et al., 2016). The researchers also suggested that compatibility has a positive relationship with the adoption of 4IR digital disruptive technology. IDT can explain the 4IR disruptive innovations, so long as the technology in IME, altering the network can change the existing business models to correspond to corporate structures radicalization (Christensen, 1997; Christensen, 2003; Gassman, 2006; Zeleny, 2009; Utesheva et al., 2016; Nyagadza, 2019b). In this chapter, the TAM is applied as the theoretical framework in deriving the link between 4IR disruptive technologies and IME. The intention to use technology is determined by three factors, namely: the personal one, which is shown by human attitude, the subjective norms that reflect the social influences, and finally, the perceived behavioral control.

Modeling Framework

When reviewing the literature and related theoretical analysis, I formulated the following conceptual model. Figure 3.1 depicts technological,

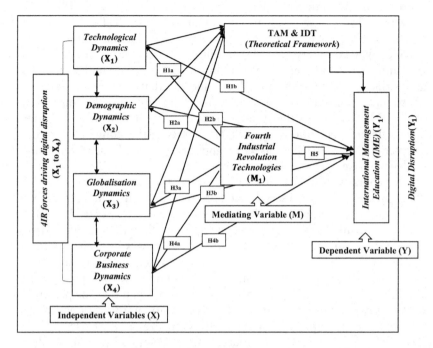

Figure 3.1 Fourth Industrial Revolution and International Management Education conceptual model.

Source: Researcher's conception (2020). Derived from literature and theoretical review.

demographic, globalization, and corporate business dynamics as independent variables, whereas the mediating variable is the 4IR technologies. Lastly, the dependent variables are international IME.

When applying the model to data, the researchers may need first to verify the absence of endogeneity through simultaneity between Y_1 and X_1. If X_1 is endogenous, an instrumental variable should be used to solve the problem. With the stated schematic conceptual model, the following propositions have been formulated in line with the future research direction:

> H1a: *Fourth Industrial Revolution technologies positively influence International Management Education.*
> H1b: *Technological Dynamics positively influence Fourth Industrial Revolution technologies.*
> H2a: *Fourth Industrial Revolution technologies influence positively Demographic Dynamics.*
> H2b: *Demographic Dynamics positively influence International Management Education.*

H3a: *Fourth Industrial Revolution technologies positively influence Globalization Dynamics.*

H3b: *Globalization Dynamics influence positively International Management Education.*

H4a: *Fourth Industrial Revolution technologies influence positively Corporate Business Dynamics.*

H4b: *Corporate Businesses' Dynamics influence positively International Management Education.*

H5: *Fourth Industrial Revolution technologies influence positively International Management Education.*

In line with the above research model, the following simple regression equation can be used to establish the linkages between variables, together with the structural equation modeling for building a model for testing the relationships:

$$Y_{1\&2} = \beta_0 + \beta_1 X_1 + \beta_2 X_2 + \beta_3 X_3 + \beta_4 X_4 + M_1 + u_t$$

where

Y_1 = *International Management Education (IME)*
X_1 = *Technology Dynamics*
X_2 = *Demography Dynamics*
X_3 = *Globalization Dynamics*
X_4 = *Corporate Business Dynamics*
M_1 = *Fourth Industrial Revolution (4IR) technologies*
u_t = *Unobserved error term*
* M_1 *is the mediating variable*
* $Y_{1\&2}$ *are the dependent/response variables*
* *From X_1 to X_2 represent the independent/explanatory variables*

Also, and reference to the preceding hypotheses in the modeling framework, the researcher views that an opportunity for further predictive future research can point into addressing the following thematic questions:

- How may IME colleges take advantage of the 4IR?
- How can digital disruption and digital innovation be combined to produce leverage for IME?
- How may professional and academic IME practitioners readily uptake smart technologies in the wake of digital disruption caused by the 4IR technologies?
- What could be the barriers affecting the 4IR smart technologies within IME institutions?
- How may 4IR digital disruption anecdotal feedback from industry, academic, and professional IME practitioners help produce corporate metamorphoses fit for survival?

- Can the relational approach theory be fully applied to understand 4IR digital disruption and digital innovation concepts?

Methods for Collecting and Analyzing Literature

I used a systematic literature review survey that utilized an inductive research approach. I used a qualitative analysis to collect and analyze the literature. My research used the Google search engine. The words such as '4IR,' 'IME,' 'smart technologies,' 'digital disruption,' 'digital technologies' were used to guide the search process. I continued with the verification of the identified articles in journals that have a strong reputation in the area of social media marketing: *Journal of Management Information Systems, The Journal of Strategic Information Systems, European Journal of Information Systems, MIT Sloan Management Review, Journal of Information Technology, Management Information Systems,* and others. The literature gathering was done in February 2020 and was not limited to specific years. Articles that were not related to the study area were deleted from the selection. All nonempirical items were excluded.

The search process resulted in a summation of 120 papers that the author coded subsequently. The discovered articles were heralded between 2003 and 2020. Each journal was analyzed and given codes with descriptions to find the main areas in the 120 papers. The keywords were then researched and populated into defined and identifiable strategic themes. This work was completed in tandem with the precepts and procedures of the ethnographic approach. However, the researcher used relational assumption in the literature analysis due to the complexity of the phenomenon, premised on the fact that 'something comes into play as a result of something else' (Utesheva et al., 2016). The databases were Scopus, Springer Link, and Emerald Insight through the Chartered Institute of Marketing catalog, World Cat, Congent, Routledge, CRS, SAGE open, Taylor and Francis abstracts.

Implications and Conclusion

4IR impact on IME has some predictive challenges. IME digital learning has contributed to common online learning problems (Kahne and Bowyer, 2019). Factors such as the spread of misinformation (Kahne and Bowyer, 2019), echo chambers (Kahne and Bowyer, 2019; Pariser, 2011; Nyagadza, 2019b), and incivility (Kahne and Bowyer, 2019) have aggravated the situation. Research results from a study by Wertalik (2017) unpacked that social media platforms can be used as learning channels to deliver IME. Wertalik (2017) saw that Facebook has more negative influence (topping at 35% compared to others) among the students at Pamplin College of Business Marketing, Virginia, USA. The issue depicts that social media platforms have expanded opportunities for management education, learning, and interactivity. Research suggests the digital natives' generations use online educational technology to exchange ideas, feelings, information, visuals, and money at a remarkable rate during school hours (Wang, Chen, and Liang, 2011; Wertlik, 2017). Wright and Hinson argued that in the USA, the emergence of educational blog spots has changed how IME students interact (53% in 2007 and 69% by 2008%), (numbers continue to rise even in future trajectorially forecasts).

The rise in blogs' emergence is because youthful IME college students have better leverage power of online and digital publicity engagement (Khane and Bowyer, 2019; Mihailidis, 2018). Although the students are more involved in online activities (Khane and Bowyer, 2019), there is significant evidence that many of them are disengaged from civic and political life; most of them rarely create and circulate political content (Khane and Bowyer, 2019; Cohen et al., 2011). With this, Reich and Solomon (2008) offer some tips and suggestions to organizations and individuals on how to use the new media (4IR) technologies in harnessing useful IME.

The influence of the emerging 4IR technologies will require an overhaul and reconsideration of the IME curriculum to comprehend and thoughtfully analyze and predict the trends related to the economic ecosystem's

Table 3.3 International Management Education (IME) skills needed in tandem with the Fourth Industrial Revolution (4IR) emerging technologies

Available in 2018	Trending by 2022	Declining by 2022
Analytical thinking and innovation	Analytical thinking and innovation	Manual dexterity, endurance, and precision
Complex problem-solving	Active learning and learning strategies	Memory, verbal, auditory, and spatial abilities
Critical thinking and analysis	Creativity, originality, and initiative	Management of financial, material resources
Active learning and learning strategies	Technology design and programming	Technology installation and maintenance
Creativity, originality, and initiative	Critical thinking and analysis	Reading, writing, math, and active listening
Attention to detail, trustworthiness	Complex problem-solving	Management of personnel
Emotional intelligence	Leadership and social influence	Quality control and safety awareness
Reasoning, problem-solving, and ideation	Emotional intelligence	Coordination and time management
Leadership and social influence	Reasoning, problem-solving, and ideation	Visual, auditory, and speech abilities
Coordination and time management	Systems analysis and evaluation	Technology use, monitoring, and control

Source: World Economic Forum (2018).

sociopolitical systems. With the growing use of technology, AI may bring robots as tutors. The advance means human interactions shall be limited across the IME learning processes. The learning processes shall be refined, reimagined, and enriched to match the demands, as indicated in Table 3.3. There shall be a symbiotic relationship between IME and the emerging 4IR technologies. Conclusively, the revolution shall make the students, professionals, and academics to be able to develop teams, interconnected globally, with a common culture, for sustainable development.

References

Anderson, P., Jané-Llopis, E. & Cooper, C. 2011. "The Imperative of Wellbeing". *Stress & Health*, 27(5). https://doi.org/10.1002/smi.1433

African Development Bank (AfDB). 2019. *African Development Bank (AfDB) Annual Report 2019*. Accessed (20/11/20). www.afdb.org/en/documents/annual-report-2019

Amodu, L., Omojola, O., Okorie, N., Adeyeye, B. and Adesina. E. 2019. "Potentials of Internet of things for effective public relations activities: Are professionals ready?" *Cogent Business & Management*, 6, p. 1683951. https://doi.org/10.1080/23311975.2019.1683951.

Balmer, J. M. T. 2001. "Corporate identity, corporate branding and corporate marketing-seeing through the fog". *European Journal of Marketing*, 35(3/4), pp. 248–291.

Balmer, J. M. T. & Gray, E. R. 2003. "Corporate brands: what are they? What of them?" *European Journal of Marketing*, 37(7/8), pp. 972–997.

Balmer, J.M.T. & Greyser, S. A. 2006. "Managing the multiple identities of the corporation". *California Management Review*, 44(3), pp. 72–86.

Bauernhansl, T., Ten Hompel, M., & Vogel-heuser, B. 2014. *Industrie 4.0 in produktion, automatisierung und logistik* (1st ed.). Wiesbaden, Germany: Springer Vieweg.

Bouchard, B. 2010. Transaction costs. *Encyclopedia of Quantitative Finance*. John Wiley.

Bower, J. L. and Christensen, C. M. 1995. Disruptive Technologies: Catching the Wave. Accessed 21/11/2020. https://hbr.org/1995/01/disruptive-technologies-catching-the-wave

Brown, J. S and Duguid, P. 1994. "Borderline issues: Social and material aspects of design". *Human-Computer Interaction*, 9(1), pp. 3–36.

Caruana, A. 1997. "Corporate reputation: Concept and measurement". *Journal of Product & Brand Management*, 6(2), pp. 109–118.

Ching, H. L. and Ellis P. 2004. "Marketing in Cyberspace: What Factors Drive E-Commerce Adoption?" *Journal of Marketing Management* 20(3–4), pp. 409–429.

Christensen, C. M. 1997. *The Innovator's Dilemma: When New Technologies Cause Great Firms to Fail*. Boston, MA: Harvard Business Press.

Christensen, C. M. 2003. *The Innovator's Solution: Creating and Sustaining Successful Growth*. Boston, MA: Harvard Business Press.

Cohen, Tom, Claire Colebrook, and J. Hillis Miller. 2011. *Theory and the Disappearing Future: On de Man, on Benjamin*. Routledge: London.

Danila, C., Stegaru, G., Stanescu, A. M. and Serbanescu, C. 2016. Web-service based architecture to support SCM context-awareness and interoperability. *Journal of Intelligent Manufacturing*, 27(1), pp. 73–82.

de Chernatony, L. 1999. "Brand management through narrowing the gap between brand identity and brand reputation". *Journal of Marketing Management*, 15, pp. 157–179.

Dozier, D., Shen, H., Sweetser, K. and Barker, V. 2016. "Demographics and internet behaviours as predictors of active public". *Public Relations Review*, 42, pp. 82–90, DOI: 10.1016/j.pubrev.2015.11.006.

Ducey, A. J. 2013. *Predicting Tablet Computer Use: An Extended Technology Acceptance Model*. Accessed November 25, 2019. http://scholarcommons.usf.edu/etd/4471

Eberl, M. and Schwaiger, M. 2005. "Corporate reputation: Disentangling the effects on financial performance". *European Journal of Marketing*, 39(7/8), pp. 838–854.

Fombrun, C. J. 1998. "Indices of corporate reputation: An analysis of media rankings and social monitors' ratings". *Corporate Reputation Review*, 1(4), pp. 327–340.

Gassman, O. 2006. "Opening up the innovation process: towards an agenda". *R & D Management*, 36(3). https://doi.org/10.1111/j.1467-9310.2006.00437.x

Harris, F. and DeChernatony, L. 2001. "Corporate branding and corporate brand performance". *European Journal of Marketing*, 35(3), pp. 441–456.

Harrison, D. A, Price, K. H. & Bell, M. P. 1998. "Beyond Relational Demography: Time and the Effects of Surface- and Deep-Level Diversity on Work Group Cohesion". *The Academy of Management Journal*, 41(1), pp. 96–107.

Hatch, M. J. and Schultz, M. 2003. "Bringing the corporation into corporate branding". *European Journal of Marketing*, 37(7/8), pp. 1041–1064.

Helms, S. 2007. "One reputation or many? Comparing stakeholders' perceptions of corporate reputation". *Corporate Reputation*, 12(3), pp. 238–254.

Heyman, T., Rensbergen, B. V., Storm, G., Hutchinson, K. A. and De Deyne, S. 2014. "The influence of working memory load on semantic priming". *Journal of Experimental Psychology: Learning, Memory, and Cognition Impact Factor*, 41(3), pp. 911–920. https://doi.org/10.1037/xlm0000050

Kahne. J and Bowyer, B. 2019. "Can media literacy education increase digital engagement in politics?" *Learning, Media and Technology*, 44(2), pp. 211–224. DOI: 10.1080/17439884.2019.1601108.

Kapferer, J. N. 1997. *Strategic Brand Management: Creating and Sustaining Brand Equity Long Term*. (2nd ed.). London: Kogan Page.

Kay, J. 2006. *Managing Behaviour in the Early Years*. London, Oxford: Bloomsbury. ISBN: 9780826484659.

Keller, K. L. 2003. "Brand Synthesis: The Multidimensionality of Brand Knowledge". *Journal of Consumer Research* 29 (4): pp. 595–600. https://doi.org/10.1086/346254

Kim, B. 2020. *Moving Forward with Digital Disruption: What Big Data, IoT, Synthetic Biology, AI, Blockchain, and Platform Businesses Mean to Libraries*. Chicago: American Library Association. ISBN: 978-0-8389-4673-2. DOI: https://doi.org/10.5860/ltr.56n2.

Knox, S. and Bickerton, D. 2003. "The six conventions of corporate branding". *European Journal of Marketing*, 37 (7/8), pp. 998–1016.

Kotler, P. (2010). *Principles of Marketing*. Upper Saddle River, NJ: Pearson.

Kumar, C. R. (2013). *Research Methodology*. New Delhi: APH.

Kurzweil, R. (2005). *The Singularity Is Near: When humans transcend biology*. Penguin Books. ISBN: 9780143037880.

Lee, I. 2015. "The Internet of Things (IoT): Applications, investments, and challenges for enterprises". *Business Horizons*, 58(4), pp. 431–440.

Manyika, J. 2013. *Disruptive Technologies: Advances that Will Transform Life, Business, and the Global Economy*. McKinsey Global Institute, May. www.mckinsey.com/insights/business_technology/disruptive_technologies.

McAfee, A. and Brynjolfsson, E. 2017. *Machine, Platform, Crowd: Harnessing Our Digital Future*. New York: W. W. Norton, p. 64.

Micheler, S, Goh, Y. M. and Lohse, N. 2019. "Innovation landscape and challenges of smart technologies and systems – A European perspective". *Production & Manufacturing Research*, 7(1), pp. 503–528. https://doi.org/10.1080/21693277.2019.1687363.

Mihailidis, P. 2018. "Civic media literacies: Re-imagining engagement for civic intentionality". *Learning, Media, and Technology*, 43(2), pp. 152–164. (Published online 6 February 2018).

Moore, G. A. 1991. *Crossing the Chasm: Marketing and Selling High-Tech Goods to Mainstream Customers*. New York: Harper Business.

Morley, J. 2016. "Macro-Finance Linkages". *Journal of Economic Surveys*, 30(4). https://doi.org/10.1111/joes.12108

Nyagadza, B. 2019a. "Responding to change and customer value improvement: Pragmatic advice to banks". *The Marketing Review (TMR)*, 19(3–4), pp. 235–252. https://doi.org/10.1362/146934719X15774562877719.

Nyagadza, B. 2019b. "Conceptual model for financial inclusion development through agency banking in competitive markets". *Africanus: Journal of Development Studies*, 49(2), pp. 2663–6522. https://doi.org/10.25159/2663-6522/6758.

Nyagadza, B. 2020. "Search engine marketing and social media marketing predictive trends". *Journal of Digital Media & Policy*. DOI: https://doi.org/10.1386/jdmp_00027_1.

Nyagadza, B., Kadembo, E. M. and Makasi, A. 2019. "An application of impression management theory on corporate storytelling for branding in examining internal stakeholders' corporate brand perceptions". *The Retail and Marketing Review*. 15(2), pp. 39–50.

Nyagadza, B., Kadembo E. M. and Makasi. A. 2020a. "Exploring internal stakeholders' emotional attachment & corporate brand perceptions through corporate storytelling for branding". *Cogent Business & Management*. DOI: 10.1080/23311975.2020.1816254.

Nyagadza, B., Kadembo E. M. and Makasi. A. 2020b. "Corporate storytelling for branding: underpropping or thwarting internal stakeholders' optimistic corporate brand perceptions". *Cogent Social Sciences* (under review).

Nyagadza, B, Kabonga, I., Hlungwani, P. M., Chigora, F and Rukasha, T. 2020c. Fourth Industrial Revolution (4IR) implications on African sovereignty, ownership and control of resources, book chapter accepted for publication in Nhemachena, A. and Kangira, J. (Eds), *Africa When National Liberation Movements Are Destroyed: Hope or Existential Angst in the 21st Century*. Cameroon: Langaa Publishers.

Ordoobadi, S. M. 2011. "Application of ANP methodology in evaluation of advanced technologies". *Journal of Manufacturing Technology Management*, 23(2), pp. 229–252.

Pariser, E. 2011. "Beware online 'filter bubbles' ". *TEDvideo*, 8(58), filmed March 2011. www.ted.com/talks/eli_pariser_beware_online_filter_bubbles.

Petrovici, M. A. (2014). E-Public Relations: Impact and Efficiency. A case study. *Procedia - Social and Behavioral Sciences*, 141, pp. 79–84.

Philips, D. and Young, P. 2009. *Online Public Relations: A Practical Guide to Developing an Online Strategy in the World of Social Media*. (2nd ed.). London: Kogan Page.

Reich, B. and Solomon, D. 2008. *Media Rules: Mastering Today's Technology*. Hoboken, NJ: John Wiley.

Rogers, E. M. (1993). *Diffusion of Innovations*. 4th ed. New York: Free Press.

Rojewski, J. W and Hill, R. B. 2017. "A framework for 21st-century career-technical and workforce education curricula". *Peabody Journal of Education*, 92(2), pp. 180–191.

Schwab, K. 2016. *The Fourth Industrial Revolution*. New York: Currency. pp. 6–7. www.weforum.org/about/the-fourth-industrial-revolution-by-klaus-schwab

Scott, C. 2010. The Enduring Appeal of 'Learning Styles', *Australian Journal of Education*, 54(1). https://doi.org/10.1177%2F000494411005400102

Spotts. H. E. & Weinberger, M. G. 2010. "Marketplace footprints: connecting marketing communication and corporate brands". *European Journal of Marketing*, 44(5), pp. 591–609. https://doi.org/10.1108/03090561011032289

Tankosic, M. and Trifunovic, D. 2016. Development of Cultural Institutions through Implementation of Service Innovation, Proceedings of the 5th International Conference on Applied Economics, Business and Development (AEBD '13), Chania, Crete Island, Greece, 2013, pp. 161–166.

Teo. G. 2010. "A Critical Assessment of Determinants of Financial Deepening in Nigeria (1970–2010)". *Interdisciplinary Journal of Contemporary Research in Business* 4(10).

Teo, T., Ursava, F. O. and Bahcekapili E. 2011. "Efficiency of the Technology Acceptance Model to Explain Pre-Service Teachers' Intention to Use Technology". *International Journal of Information and Learning Technology* 28(2), pp. 93–101. https://doi.org/10.1108/10650741111117798

Tripsas, M. (2009). "Technology, Identity, and Inertia through the Lens of 'The Digital Photography Company' ". *Organization Science*, 20(2), pp. 441–460.

Utesheva, A., Cecez-Kecmanovic, D. & Simpson, J. R. 2016. "Identity metamorphoses in digital disruption: a relational theory of identity". *European Journal of Information Systems*, 25, pp. 344–368. https://doi.org/10.1057/ejis.2015.19

Van Der Velden, C., Bil, C., and Xu, X. 2012. "Adaptable methodology for automation application development". *Advanced Engineering Informatics*, 26(2), pp. 231–250.

van Riel, C. B. M. and Balmer, J. M. T. 1997. "Corporate identity: The concept, its measurement and management". *European Journal of Marketing*, 31(5/6), pp. 340–355.

Vercic, D., Vercic, A. and Sriramesh, K. 2015. "Looking for digital in public relations". *Public Relations Review*, 41(2), pp. 142–152. DOI:10.1016/j.pubrev.2014.12.002

Wang, Y. 2015. "Incorporating social media in public relations: A synthesis of social media-related public relations research". *Public Relations Journal*, 9(3), pp. 1–14.

Wang, Q., Chen, W. and Liang, Y. 2011. *The effects of social media on college student (Paper 5)*. *MBA Student Scholarship*. Retrieved from http://scholarsarchive.jwu.Edu/mba_student/5

Wartick, S. L. (2002). "Measuring Corporate Reputation: Definition and Data". *Business & Society*, 41(4). https://doi.org/10.1177%2F0007650302238774

Wertalik D, 2017. "Social media and building a connected college". *Cogent Business & Management*, 4, p. 1320836. https://doi.org/10.1080/23311975.2017.1320836.

World Economic Forum (WEF). 2018. *The Future of Jobs Report 2018. Insight Report*. Geneva, Switzerland: World Economic Forum.

Xu, M., David, J. M. and Kim, S. H. 2018. "The Fourth Industrial Revolution; opportunities and challenges". *International Journal of Finance Research*, 9(2), pp. 90–95.

Young, R. 2009. "Social media: How new forms of communications are changing job search and career management". *Be Heard. Newsletter of the Toronto Chapter of the International Association of Business Communicators*. January–February.

Younus, M., Hu, L., Yuqing, F., and Yong, C. P. 2009. "Manufacturing execution system for a subsidiary of aerospace manufacturing industry". Proceeding – 2009 *International Conference on Computer and Automation Engineering ICCAE 2009* (pp. 208–212). Bangkok, Thailand.

Zeleny, M. 2009. "Technology and high technology: Support net and barriers to innovation". *Advanced Management Systems*, 1(1), pp. 8–21.

4 Technological Frame and Best Praxis in the Age of Artificial Intelligence

Toyoko Sato

Introduction

Artificial intelligence (AI) is a phenomenon that gives rise to various discourses with its operational, managerial, and societal practices today and its capacity and capability in the future. Because it is entwined with many fields and perspectives and its fast-changing nature, defining AI is not easy. In this respect, reading the earliest definition of AI is helpful to understand its intention. McCarthy et al. (2006) wrote that AI could simulate any human intelligence feature, solve human problems, and improve human solutions. From the point of its inception, AI was envisioned to be a human extension—it is purported to stimulate and promote a way of *thinking* as much as possible in human life.

Today, AI is seen as both a miracle and a threat (Cooley, 1980; Müller, 2016; Petropoulos, 2018; Yudkowsky, 2008). It can be a good thing because, as many experts advocate, human errors are substantially reduced when programming is done correctly. It can be much faster than previous technology. For example, manufacturing automation has realized its maximum functional efficiency. Using extensive data, AI can perform faster and more accurate predictive analyses.

On the other hand, others point out that it is a threat or even a curse, as so many jobs are lost to newly deployed AI systems. The list of human jobs that will eventually surrender to AI is increasing ceaselessly. Furthermore, it is arguably problematic, as AI is one of the outcomes of the accumulating of economic power, which tends to favor the societal majority or privileged class and ignores economically disadvantaged people. While the two conditional words, opportunities, and threat, are opposites, they are discussed simultaneously and inseparably, appearing as the opposite sides of the same coin. In connection to technology, the opportunities and threats are also the basis and drivers of international management education, which involves complex interactions among goods, information, innovation, human resources, and discourses across countries and industries concerning educational policies and practices.

It is commonly assumed that developing and controlling the latest technology triumphs over productive technology and relevant business in this context. Consequently, this logic presumes that technology inevitably influences and alters our society locally, as well as globally. This so-called *technological determinism* can be conceived within a techno-economic paradigm. Seeing how information technology has expanded its network and brought new experiences to production styles and consumer behaviors and lifestyles, we cannot deny that this techno-economic paradigm impacts society. However, the critical question remains: how will the techno-economic paradigm identify people and society in connection to technology? In particular, in viewing this question as a managerial issue, we must ask what the basis of management and leadership will be in this new era and whether any guiding principles can be used to lead international management education. By posing these questions, my goal in this chapter is to discuss historical and current frameworks connected to technology, particularly AI.

As conceptual, interdisciplinary writing, I have organized it into five sections. First, the concept of technological determinism is introduced. Its historical dimension is explained briefly through foundational thinkers of technological determinism, such as Marx and Veblen. After that, Schumpeter's theory of critical destruction (1942), one of the most vital conceptual frameworks of technological determinism, is discussed.

Second, I will introduce concepts from science, technology, and society studies (STS), which situate science and technology within their societal contexts (Bijker, & Pinch, 2012; Callon & Law, 1997; Latour, 2013). The techno-social views from STS problematize and compliment a weakness in the techno-economic paradigm's ideology. Specifically, the STS's techno-societal approach challenges determinism by identifying who the relevant groups/actors are in technological advancement and who has or retains the power to decide technology deployment.

Third, AI and its environment are discussed in connection to a report by the Organization for Economic Co-operation and Development (OECD, 2019a,b) and the G20 Osaka agreement (2019). Here, we focus on AI issues, particularly its accountability and liability in business and society within the global arena. AI issues lead to the question of authenticity. While AI may speed up, filling the trust gap in trust, the trust itself is built through human efforts made in organizational decision-making. I will argue that appropriate decision-making plays a crucial role in building authenticity; the importance and accurate measure of such decision-making remain grounded in ethics and social responsibility.

Fourth, Bernard Lonergan's insight-based critical realism is introduced. Lonergan's transcendental precepts will be discussed as a basis for authenticity testing. In the final discussion section, I will summarize the theories above as a techno triangulation that consists of the techno-economic concerns, techno-social concerns, and Lonergan's transcendental norms.

Technological Determinism

Technology has long been a seminal impact in studies regarding industry, labor, and society. Historically, technological determinism has been linked to the theory of productive forces expounded in German Ideology written in 1846 by Karl Marx and Friedrich Engels. They noted that technology changes the intensity of productivity and ideology and culture technology introduced. Although technological advances can be the basis of social change and while technology can function as a means to liberate serfdom, at the same time, adequate food and drink, housing, and clothing, and other political necessities are required to achieve successful liberation.

Moreover, according to Marx (1972), technology can cause *alienation*, which is a condition of estrangement, in this case, from purported and celebrated humanity: aspects of this area linked to consciousness and self-actualization. In particular, manual labor and low-wage workers become alienated under a capitalist regime, where labor exploitations are practically and legally systemized. The workers can neither enjoy their human nature nor benefit from the very products they labored to produce in the system. Nevertheless, technology remains a crucial variable and driver in the design and can certainly be the fundamental variable for economic and social change.

The term *technological determinism* is known from Thorstein Veblen, who connected technology with a ceremonial aspect. Seeing scientists and engineers playing active parts in society and contributing to the industrial production system and its improvement in the United States, Veblen (1899) considered that human existence could be described and conditioned by material existence. The material condition changes our lifestyle and mode of thinking. For instance, having an automobile at the turn of the 19th century was apparently for the leisure class. Technology is a factor of endorsing socially conspicuous economic behavior as an American institution in a consumer society. Indeed, this view of Veblen's entails an irony concerning the prominent aspect of consumption. His idea of evolving technology, however, appears not to be so ironic. Technology is treated as an independent and relatively neutral entity. It seems to be entrusted in the hands "of the people." Nevertheless, Veblen's underlying pessimistic tone is a tenet because individuals' autonomy and agency are somewhat compromised in his thesis.

Creative Destruction

The conceptual tenet of technological determinism has emerged from time to time and, in our age of AI, overtly, and covertly. Joseph Schumpeter's theory of creative destruction is such an early and continuous exemplar in innovation. According to Schumpeter (1942), successful innovations emerge powerfully from within an economic structure and revolutionize the industry in question with continuous innovative power. The types of invention applicable to creative destruction can be roughly grouped into five. They are new production processes, new products, new materials/resources, new markets, and new organizational forms. Over the process of innovation, an old method of doing things becomes obsolete and no longer competitive. When the new method dominates the market, the market itself will be metabolized, and eventually, the innovation as creative destruction destroys the old model.

While Schumpeter's theory was constructed in the early half of the 20th century, it is still inspiring in various ways today. For instance, music streaming services changed music production, publishing, and distribution industries (Sato, 2014). The significant first and the pivotal creative move was by the peer-to-peer file-sharing software Napster established in 1999 by Shawn Fanning, John Fanning, and Sean Parker. Although it went bankrupt in 2001 due to a lawsuit by the Recording Industry Association of America (RIAA), the heavy metal band Metallica, and others over copyright and intellectual property law violations, creating peer-to-peer file sharing triggered Apple's iTunes.

Interestingly, Sean Parker became the first CEO of Facebook and a significant investor and board member for the then-new music streaming service Spotify. The creative destruction processes, in this case, could be tracked in the following steps: (1) music tapes made vinyl obsolete, (2) compact discs made music tapes obsolete, (3) peer-to-peer free file sharing technology made music compact discs obsolete, and (4) music streaming made music downloading obsolete. Also, we can add that (5) the Sony Walkman made room stereo components less attractive in terms of usable spaces. Then, (6) iTunes and the iPod made the Sony Walkman less attractive, owing to the volume of accessible music and the prices of tapes and CDs; and (7) the music-connecting iPhone made iPods less in demand. Now, music is stored in the cloud for consumers, where AI is strategically connected to marketing and user analytics.

From this perspective, we should observe creative destruction as both creative and destructive in processes. Schumpeter did not mention that the creative process develops not always linearly but rather in a *loop* and *spiral* to some extent in some industries. The spiral nature is because an approach that was seen as obsolete yesterday appeals to today's consumers' eyes. For instance, in the music industry, vinyl, which was seen as old-fashioned, is now something attractive as a collector's item and serious listeners (RIAA, 2019). Furthermore, while the 2020 statistics are expected to be low because of the COVID-19 lockdowns, live music tickets increased continuously over the last ten years, according to the International Association of the Phonographic Industry (2019). However, the very music ticket bookings now rely significantly on automation. Nearly every stage of creating vinyl records also can use automation today (VF Magazine, 2016). Thus, while consumer behavior could return to that of previous lifestyles, the technology supporting these behaviors often takes the course of a creative loop/spiral.

The Social Construction of Technology (SCOT)

Concerning the decision-making process for STS, social determinism takes the opposite view from technological determinism. Social determinism is a research stream that examines moments of science and technology in relation to society. This approach queries if technologies are beneficial for users and society in light of political, economic, and mercantile interests.

A social determinism perspective asserts that society and users should be the main power that shapes science and technology. This view expects technology to be open to external forces and its deployment negotiable with these forces. However, science is not wholly neutral and remains susceptible to biases. Civil groups could and should be included in the technological actualization process to avoid discriminatory policies related to technology (MacKenzie & Wajcman, 1985).

One of the representative studies in this area is the *Forces of Production* by David Noble (1984), which is about the American machine tool industry's postwar automation. Noble explains that at the beginning of computerization, entangled factors, such as politics, foreign diplomacy, economic power, such research universities as MIT, and the military-industrial complex, impacted industrial automation and technological designs. It shows how numerical control was chosen and how unemployment remained a structural problem in the United States.

The emphasis in Noble's work was more on technology than science. The technology emphasis paralleled other *society shapes science and technology* streams called the SCOT (Bijker, Hughes, & Pinch, 1987) and the Actor-Network Theory (ANT; Callon, 1986; Latour, 1987). While both focus more on technological artifacts than science, SCOT emphasizes the actualization and usage of artifacts, while the ANT concerns such artifacts' networks. Its major theoretical development in SCOT entails three distinctive features: *interpretative flexibility, relevant social groups,* and *seamless web* (Fuglsang, 2001; Klein & Kleinman, 2002; Jones & Bissell, 2011). The term interpretive flexibility describes the plasticity of technology during its beginning stage.

Technology goes back and forth in terms of designing, developing, and marketizing artifacts. Interpretative flexibility suggests that technology is not merely a linear progress. In each process, technology encounters relevant social groups and should be assessed and adjusted to meet societal needs. In a SCOT analysis, social groups include the scientists and engineers who design technological artifacts, skilled and unskilled workers connected to technological development, distributers who deliver in the supply chain, retailers, and consumers. Also, media (including social media today), educators, and investors can be included in this network.

If a group wishes to slow down technology, they will voice their concerns and intervene. Another group may find inconveniences or deficiencies in technology and demand it be altered for their convenience. Science and technology are not confrontative or antagonistic SCOT components. According to Bijker (1995), they should exist in a seamless web, where STS are integrated. The democratization of technology occurs in this seamless web as associative democracy. Public organizations, private companies, and social groups dialogue with one another and negotiate the outcome of technology and its deployment. Relevant groups' discourses help to form societal discourses for and judgments of the technology in question.

SCOT is an interactive approach for STS studies, but there are SCOT criticisms. The most notable is from Langdon Winner (1993), who asserted that SCOT's single-case method, like Bijker's (1995) bicycle study is not sufficient to generalize technological artifacts and their societal position. Yet, suppose a theoretical view can help capture a phenomenon and articulate its structural constituency from myriad complications and entanglements surrounding technological artifacts. In that case, SCOT analysis offers a new perspective that was not manifested before.

AI and First Principles

In 1950, Alan Turing asked, "Can machines think?" Turing developed a test to examine whether a machine's intelligent ability was equivalent to that of humans. The Turing test created the belief that any machine passing the Turing test can be thought of as having become conscious. McLuhan (1964, pp. 383–384) discusses this further, with emphasis on *our*.

> Any process that approaches instant interrelation of a total field tends to raise itself to the level of conscious awareness, so that computers seem to "think." ...... Obviously, they can be made to simulate the process of consciousness, just as our electric global networks now begin to simulate the condition of our central nervous system. But a conscious computer would still be one that was extension of our consciousness, as a telescope is an extension of our eyes, or as a ventriloquist's dummy is an extension of the ventriloquist.

In 2020, 70 years after the Turing question, we ask what are specifically human beings? Hammond (2018), a computer scientist, stated that they are emotion, creativity, humor, intuition, and consciousness. Hammond explained that intuition could decide without knowing why and consciousness is the state or quality of awareness of our thoughts. These two concepts both oppose and complement one another. Hammond maintained that some portions of intuition and consciousness are what AI already has or can simulate.

Hammond's argument, however, raises another question. When a machine acquires consciousness, how can it have, or should we even consider it to have rights? To what extent should AI be recognized for its accountability and liability? When auto-driving cars or drones cause traffic accidents, who is responsible? This question is not for science fiction but real life, including business activities. For instance, in 2018, Air New Zealand called for stricter regulations of drones after its aircraft, and a drone had a near miss just five meters away from the aircraft, while drones are restricted to keep at least a 4-kilometer distance in New Zealand (BBC, 2018). If something happens, is it the drone's owner who is responsible or the designer/developer of the drone or the drone operator if it is a case of piloting error?

Then, how can we avoid judgmental biases when AI's deep learning is based on available data from our often-biased environment? Another example is a recruiting software developed by Amazon.com, aiming to find top talents for recruiting services. Amazon.com was obliged to abandon the software that it had been developing since 2014. According to Reuters, "[T]he company's experimental hiring tool used artificial intelligence to give job candidates scores ranging from one to five / much like shoppers rate products on Amazon" (Reuters, 2018). Amazon found that the software favored men over women due to the existing data for this program's machine learning. The gender preference reflects our given societal biases, which are often connected to the patriarchy. According to Sato (2011), this trend is embedded in our society and often highly sophisticated. It usually wears a mask of the liberal over the patriarchy. In this vein, it was fortunate that Amazon noticed the face behind the mask and scrapped its outcome.

Still, not all outcomes will be like that of Amazon's software; automation may continue to reproduce discrimination and biases. The anomalies have become a global concern. OECD promotes awareness of this, as manifested in "the OECD Council Recommendations on Artificial Intelligence" (OECD AI principles) in 2019. Below are five principles identified in the recommendation:

- AI should benefit people and the planet by driving inclusive growth, sustainable development, and well-being.
- AI systems should be designed in a way that respects the rule of law, human rights, democratic values, and diversity, and they should include appropriate safeguards—for example, enabling human intervention where necessary—*to ensure a fair and just society.*
- There should be *transparency and responsible disclosure* around AI systems to ensure that people understand AI-based outcomes and challenge them.
- AI systems must function in a robust, secure, and safe way throughout their life cycles and *potential risks* should be continually assessed and managed.

- Organizations and individuals developing, deploying, or operating AI systems should be held accountable for their proper functioning according to the above principles (OECD, 2019a, italics added).

The principles were discussed with more than 50 expert groups consisting of people from 20 countries. Forty-two countries adapted the recommendation at the G20 2019 Osaka Summit, and it identifies these five objectives for governments.

- Facilitate public and private investment in research and development to spur innovation in trustworthy AI.
- Foster accessible AI ecosystems with digital infrastructure and technologies and mechanisms to share data and knowledge.
- Ensure a policy environment that will open the way to the deployment of *trustworthy* AI systems.
- Empower people with the skills for AI and support workers for a fair transition.
- Cooperate across borders and sectors to progress on responsible stewardship of *trustworthy* AI (OECD, 2019a, italics added).

In the recommendation, there is a term, *AI system life cycle*. It involves the: "i) 'design, data and models'; which is a context-dependent sequence encompassing planning and design, data collection and processing, as well as model building; ii) 'verification and validation'; iii) 'deployment'; and iv*)* 'operation and monitoring'" (OECD, 2019b). Another vital term is *AI actors*, who are defined as "those who play an active role in the AI system lifecycle, including organizations and individuals that deploy or operate AI" (OECD, 2019b). Based on the OECD recommendations, the G20 Osaka Summit reached an agreement that "AI actors should be *accountable* for the proper functioning of AI systems and the respect of the above principles, based on their roles, the context, and consistent with state of the art" (G20 Osaka, 2019, italics added).

Certainly, receptive users are not included in the category of AI actors. Though, individuals or organizations who are active in the AI system life cycle are recognized as liable and accountable. In other words, AI itself is not recognized as responsible or accountable here. As a cross-border system, the AI system life cycle assumes human beings or organizations made by human beings should be liable and responsible. Nevertheless, the term AI actors evoke the ANT (Callon & Latour, 1992; Law, 1992), where *actors* are identified as both human and non-human beings—they are treated as equal in the ANT. There is a parallel or even sign in the G20 document that Bruno Latour's nonhuman actors are recognized as similar to human actors; the global governance of AI is the global governance of AI actors in the AI system life cycle.

Theoretically, one of the most critical issues is to identify relevant stakeholders in technological advancement. Regardless of the tone, the tenet of technological determinism emphasizes science and technology, while science and technology and society studies maintain the social factor as fundamental. Within the latter, the point of SCOT, on the other hand, was that the evident web should be a seamless configuration through negotiations among STS. In the case of ANT, relevant stakeholders include non-human actors. Seeing nonhuman actors as a stakeholder is more accepted when we discuss current terminology: the Internet of Things (IoT). In the beginning, IoT was described and analyzed in relation to business areas, such as supply chains and logistics. Today, it appears to expand to our digital life (Ashton, 2009), including military, data security, and machine-to-machine communications. AI will offer various automated techniques and skills for accountants, auditors, and the process of corporate governance. Additionally, blockchain technology is expected to help this process by linking to algorithmic automation.

AI Actors and International Management Education

In some medical areas, such as cancer detection and diagnosis, AI is considered more accurate than human physicians (Walsh, 2020). There will soon be counseling services with AI therapists and consulting services with AI lawyers, against whom human therapists and human attorneys may compete in the market. Today, many stock investment recommendations are already analyzed and written by an automation.

AI also shows significant momentum in the areas of culture and cultural industry. For instance, AI can compose not only simple songs but also complex and lengthy symphonies now. Through deep learning, dead artists, such as Glenn Gould, have been simulated with new piano music that he never played in his lifetime (Bloomberg, 2019). Hibari Misora has been manufactured with new Japanese pop songs (Businesswire, 2019). Behind these media-worthy scenes, automation is invading our life quietly. We are no longer sure which AI made background music for cinemas and commercial films.

One of the most popular stories in this context happened in 2016. AlphaGo, developed by Google DeepMind, is a problem-solving software and computer program for the table game called Go. Go involves two players with black and white stones. It is considered the most complex of human games. Until the early 2010s, there was no sign that AI could win against human champions. However, AlphaGo acquired the game skills and won against a Chinese professional player in 2015. The win was a significant threshold for AlphaGo. The next year, when AlphaGo challenged Lee Sedol, the 18-time world Go champion in 2016, AlphaGo won by 4:1. The following year, the AI challenged another world-class Go player and proceeded to win. These wins showed how AI reached the level of specific human achievement, which is an achievement of human endeavor that should be celebrated. Nevertheless, it also implies AlphaGo as a shadow or threat to human ingenuity and limitation. As reported, Lee

Sedol voluntarily retired from the professional Go association because, among other reasons, he lost hope to continue as a professional game player of the board game.

Our natural question is: what is next? AI developers and scientists, and a part of society agree that the expected answer appears to be a *singularity*, which is the hypothetical time when technological advancement reaches a critical mass irreversible. AI's intelligence and capability will have evolved so rapidly that human beings will be unable to control it. Like Hal in the film *2001: A Space Odyssey*, will human beings be controlled by AI? For corporate management, will organizational behaviors and strategies be determined by the deep learning of machines? There may be various answers. However, when we analyze why we ask such questions, one of the apparent reasons is connected to the shadow of threat, which is "alienation," a leitmotif of technological advancement.

Indeed, we need something that guides us in this fast-moving techno sea, and it must be more than accuracy and efficiency—it must be more than who has the stake in it. It must be how a network creates dynamism. In addition to the techno-economic and socioeconomic approaches, we need something more to lead ourselves in this dynamism. Being aware of ethics and practicing corporate social responsibility is required, the importance of which was explained in a different volume of this series (Sato in Tsang, Kazeroony, & Ellis, 2013). We did not offer earlier a path for the praxis, which can propose now: the Canadian philosopher Bernard Lonergan's insight-based critical realism, particularly the cognitive operational and dynamic structure of the mind.

In insight-based critical realism, Lonergan shares some attributes and differs from other essential thinkers of realism, such as Bhaskar (2008), Collier (1994), and Archer et al. (1998). Bhaskar (2008) maintains the approach to transcendence is to see "the objects of knowledge as the structures and mechanisms that generate phenomena; and the knowledge as produced in the social activity of science" (p. 24). Lonergan, a philosopher, theologian, and economist, viewed data of the senses and consciousness in terms of the role humans have as markers of meaning and values. Lonergan argued that humans could generalize deductively and inductively what is valuable and meaningful. STS can be seen in this light.

According to Lonergan (1992), subjectivity is not pejorative, but it "has come to denote a rejection of misconceived objectivity" (p. 219). The human subject can be attentive, intelligent, reasonable, and responsible. We are invited to judge issues for ourselves. The invitation is a part of *knowing*, which is dynamic. When one encounters something, the encountering is treated as data on four levels: experience, understanding, judgment, and decision/action. On the experience level, while our preconceptions influence our attention, our attention may yet struggle and attempt to digest data differently, especially if it is a new experience. The connection between experience, conception, and data leads to the next level, understanding the data as the result of experience. At the understanding level, we try to rationalize why the experience happened, in which way, and for what. In other words, to understand is an activity of making sense of the event or phenomenon. When one reaches this level of judgment, we are invited to judge the data; then, the final level is deciding the values and meaning for action according to responsible judgment.

Knowing can also be a self-appropriation process, which leads to Lonergan's singularly important term: *insight*. Using the story of Archimedes identifying how to weigh the density of pure gold (the Eureka moment[1]), Lonergan (1992) explains how insight comes to us:

> What we have to grasp is that insight (1) comes as a release to the tension of inquiry, (2) comes suddenly and unexpectedly, (3) is a function not of outer circumstances but of inner conditions, (4) pivots between the concrete and the abstract, and (5) passes into the habitual texture of one's mind.
>
> (p. 28)

Having insight is not the act of picturing but understanding as part of our dynamic cognitional structure, which is constituted by the above characteristics. Having insight emerges in all kinds of moments of our life: relationships, education, and business. It appears in scientific and technological moments. Lonergan also cautions about illustrative insights, which must be elementary, as whole treatises cannot be reproduced. For experts, if such crude illustrations are painful, they can bring the pain to a critical understanding of what it is or how it can be. The experience is to advance "towards an insight into insight" (Lonergan, 1992, p. 32). The negligence of merely staying with the pain risks inviting an oversight of insight or a leap from understanding.

Now that we have learned the levels of knowing and insight through Lonergan, our inquiry can return to the guideline for right praxis—the praxis to be an individual, student, educator, frontline worker, or manager. It seems to me that Lonergan's "transcendental precepts" are the answer, which state, "Be attentive, Be intelligent, Be reasonable, and Be responsible." While the precepts are expressed in the imperative form, they "point to the internal operating norms by which anyone transcends himself or herself to live in reality" (Dunne, n.d.). To be attentive, one uses observative and analytical skills to the maximum. To be intelligent about and toward things, one applies rational assessment. One is directed to a necessary form within parameters to be reasonable, on the other hand. To be responsible means that the ethics and morality of one's actions should be actualized in the entire thought process. Lonergan believed that authenticity is the quality of a person who follows these precepts (Tackney, 2018). In other words, authenticity is a characteristic acquired through dialogue with oneself and society, including managerial areas that often go beyond national borders.

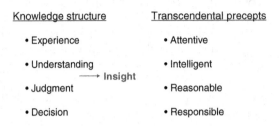

Figure 4.1 Bernard Lonergan's Praxis.

To be clear, Lonergan did not specify how we should be attentive, intelligent, reasonable, and responsible. For those who seek detailed commands, this lack of specificity might be frustrating. The frustration is, however, not the point. I think that the merit of the transcendental precepts and cognitional operation resides in their spatial-temporal, generic, and invariant. Lonergan (1904–1984) is a contemporary of McLuhan (1911–1980). In his lifetime, he saw IBM come to the forefront and Apple's inception. Although Lonergan did not discuss automation phenomena, his philosophical spectrum can be understood in this age of automation and AI. His precepts give us an essential perspective for the praxis of the era. The perspectives can be translated and appropriated for the time and the conditions in which we live and can parallel the speed of our society, science, and technology (Figure 4.1).

Discussion

This chapter's point of departure was to ask how the techno-economic paradigm identifies people and society in connection to technology and what is the praxis, or best praxis, living in the techno frame extent and emerging in society. We examined the theoretical basis of technological determinism, creative destruction, and various approaches to science, technology, and social studies to answer this. AI and AI-based automation were discussed in each section. Along with these paths, the recent policies of the OECD and G20 about AI were also discussed. Seeing the core question to be a managerial issue, we also explored Lonergan's theory of insight and the transcendental precepts. There are three points to offer by way of conclusion.

First, the term and the concept of AI actors, evident in the G20's definition of the AI and principles section in this chapter, are beginning to have momentum now and will prevail in our society; this means that the IoT will be understood and practiced more widely. The AI consciousness, accountability, and liability were also discussed and recognized as important variables in business and society, both locally and globally. We must be attentive to this development. AI actors and the IoT are constituencies of not only the techno-economic but also the socio-economic approach.

In counterpoint, my second point is that AI actors have already begun to impact our senses through the Internet and communication technology, with AI active in the area of visual and audio perception. Such impact started much earlier than commonly perceived. For instance, when Isao Tomita, a composer who used the Moom III computer from his home studio in the corner of Tokyo, introduced his sounds and music to the world in 1974, it astonished the music industry, media, and audiences. The magnitude of the musical sensation was like a tsunami at the time. Yet, by the time synthesizers became easy to access and portable, the tones of these exotic sounds became familiar because people were exposed to the sounds more often than before. Such music became part of our lifestyle. Our perception of synthesizers has been assimilated, and this assimilation, I think, was a joint effort, not only of Tomita, but also of other musicians, the music industry, media, audiences, and the Moom III and other synthesizers that followed.

Today, when we use a mobile phone, it predicts and offers the next word we might use in exchanging messages. The algorithm remembers the expression patterns of the mobile phone user and predicts when similar textual cases occur. Simultaneously, the user might have a different word/answer in mind to reply but may change their selection to that suggested by the AI from past conversations—we are already communicating with these AI actors. This fact is important because, at this time, AI will soon master; for instance, the study of human facial and bodily expressions and the emotions attached to the expressions. Then, my question is whose somatic expressions and whose ethics will be taught? If particular gestures are specific to a group and if an individual from the group does not behave normatively, what happens next? Alternatively, might an individual study behavioral norm and mimic for a particular occasion? In addition, there are research and development concentrations to teach the ethics of AI (Bostrom & Yudkowsky, 2014; Etzioni & Etzioni, 2017). Yet, whose ethics are these? How can we avoid foregrounding biases implicit in these ethics? The social constructivist way of thinking, such as SCOT, is useful for dealing with these problems. They may not offer immediate solutions, but carefully crafted questions are important to open a new horizon.

Third, it should be stated that Lonergan also discussed the issue of alienation. Marx's tenet of alienation was a criticism of industrial society, where laborers are put behind progress prosperity. Lonergan argued that alienation is caused by two things: first, not to confront resentment to know why such a feeling has emerged, and second, disregarding practice grounded in the transcendental precepts as self-transcendent. Lonergan (1992) asserted that "the basic form of ideology is a doctrine that justifies such alienation" and "From these basic forms, all others can be derived. For the basic forms corrupt the social good. As self-transcendence promotes progress, so the refusal of self-transcendence turns progress into

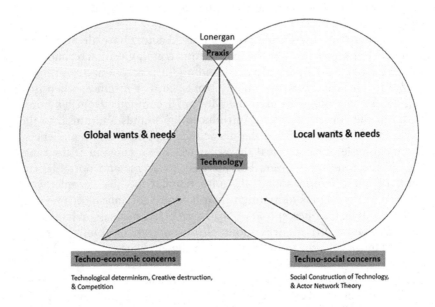

Global wants & needs

Local wants & needs

Lonergan
Praxis

Technology

Techno-economic concerns

Technological determinism, Creative destruction,
& Competition

Techno-social concerns

Social Construction of Technology,
& Actor Network Theory

Figure 4.2 Technological frame.

cumulative decline" (p. 55). Marx and Lonergan agreed with the existence of alienation, but they recognize alienation differently. For Marx, seeing industrial society's structure and its unbalanced power distribution is the first and ultimate step. For Lonergan, this step appears to result from and be made by individuals. Yet, these differences are not Either/Or, borrowing the Kierkegaard book title (2004). Today, economic disparity has not reduced but widened.

Marx and technological determinism should be taken as a critical tool for the past and present analysis. In contrast, Lonergan's approach to insight and critical realism, grounded in the precepts we have discussed, offers a reasoned and reasonable way forward for individuals and societies. Having both of these analytical tools appears to give us the strength to identify and approximate the good as the future unfolds. As Figure 4.2 illustrates, each fulfills complementary roles for the STS framework within our national and global economies.

Note

1 See Newman (2017) in National Geographic. www.nationalgeographic.com/
news/2017/05/eureka-insight-newton-archimedes-genius-science/

References

Archer, M., Bhaskar, R., Collier, A., Lawson, T. and Norrie, A. 1998. *Critical Realism: Essential Readings*. London: Routledge.

Ashton, K. 2009. That 'Internet of things' thing. *RFID Journal*, 22(7), pp. 97–114.

BBC. 2018. Air New Zealand calls for drone legislation after near miss. Last accessed in June 2020: www.bbc.com/news/world-asia-43551373

Bhaskar, R. 2008. *Dialectic: The Pulse of Freedom*. London: Routledge.

Bijker, W.E. 1995. *Of Bicycles, Bakelites, and Bulbs: Toward a Theory of Sociotechnical Change*. Cambridge, MA: MIT Press.

Bijker, W.E., Hughes, T.P. and Pinch, T.J. eds. 1987. *The Social Construction of Technological Systems: New Directions in the Sociology and History of Technology*. Cambridge, MA: MIT press.

Bijker, W.E., and Pinch, T.J. 2012. Preface to the Anniversary Edition. In W. E. Bijker, T. P. Hughes, T. Pinch, & D. G. Douglas (Eds.), *The Social Construction of Technological Systems: New Directions in the Sociology and History of Technology* (pp. xi–xxxiv). MIT Press.

Bloomberg. 2019. *Yamaha Dear Glenn Project AI System Gives Concert in Style of Legendary Pianist Glenn Gould at Ars Electronica Festival*. Last accessed in June 2020: www.bloomberg.com/press-releases/2019-10-23/yamaha-dear-glenn-project-ai-system-gives-concert-in-style-of-legendary-pianist-glenn-gould-at-ars-electronica-festival

Bostrom, N. and Yudkowsky, E. 2014. The ethics of artificial intelligence. *The Cambridge Handbook of Artificial Intelligence*, 1, pp. 316–334.

Businesswire. 2019. *Yamaha VOCALOID: AI™ Faithfully Reproduces Singing of Legendary Japanese Vocalist Hibari Misora*. Last accessed in June 2020: www.businesswire.com/news/home/20191007005420/en/Yamaha-VOCALOIDAI%E2%84%A2-Faithfully-Reproduces-Singing-Legendary-Japanese

Callon, M. 1986. The sociology of an actor-network: The case of the electric vehicle. In *Mapping the dynamics of science and technology*. London: Palgrave Macmillan. pp. 19–34.

Callon, M. and Latour, B. 1992. Don't throw the baby out with the bath school! A reply to Collins and Yearley. *Science as Practice and Culture*, 343, p. 368.

Callon, M. and Law, J. 1997. After the individual in society: Lessons on collectivity from science, technology and society. *Canadian Journal of Sociology/ Cahiers canadiens de sociologie*, 22(2), pp. 165–182.

Collier, A. 1994. *Critical Realism: An Introduction to Roy Bhaskar's Philosophy*. London: Verso.

Cooley, M. 1980. *Architect or Bee?* (p. 66). Slough: Langley Technical Services.

Dunne, T. n.d. *Bernard Lonergan (1904–1984)*. Last accessed in July 2020: www.iep.utm.edu/lonergan/

Etzioni, A. and Etzioni, O. 2017. Incorporating ethics into artificial intelligence. *The Journal of Ethics*, 21(4), pp. 403–418.

Fuglsang, L. 2001. Three perspectives in STS in the policy context. *Visions of STS: Counterpoints in Science, Technology, and Society Studies*, 35, pp. 33–49.

G20 Osaka. 2019. How Joe Biden can use confidence-building measures for military uses of AI. Last accessed in July 2020: www.mofa.go.jp/files/000486596.pdf

Hammond, K. 2018. A New Philosophy on Artificial Intelligence [Video]. TED Conferences.Last accessed in June 2020: www.youtube.com/watch?v=tr9oe2TZiJw

International Association of the Phonographic Industry. 2019. Last accessed in June 2020: www.ifpi.org/facts-and-stats.php

Jones, A. and Bissell, C. 2011. The social construction of educational technology through the use of authentic software tools. *Research in Learning Technology*, *19*(3), pp. 285–297.

Kierkegaard, S. 2004. *Either/Or: A Fragment of Life*. Harmondsworth, Middlesex: Penguin.

Klein, H.K. and Kleinman, D.L. 2002. The social construction of technology: Structural considerations. *Science, Technology, & Human Values*, 27(1), pp. 28–52.

Latour, B. 1987. *Science in action: How to follow scientists and engineers through society*. Harvard University Press.

Latour, B. 2013. Reassembling the social. An introduction to actor-network-theory. *Journal of Economic Sociology*, *14*(2), pp. 73–87.

Law, J. 1992. Notes on the theory of the actor-network: Ordering, strategy, and heterogeneity. *Systems Practice*, *5*(4), pp. 379–393.

Lonergan, B. 1992. *Insight: A Study of Human Understanding*, (Vol. 3). Toronto, Canada: University of Toronto Press.

MacKenzie, D. and Wajcman, J. 1985. *The Social Shaping of Technology*. Buckingham: Open University Press.

Marx, K. 1972. *The Marx-Engels Reader*, (Vol. 4). New York: Norton.

McCarthy, J., Minsky, M., Rochester, N. and Shannon, C. 2006. *A Proposal for the Dartmouth Summer Research Project on Artificial Intelligence*, August 31, 1955. *AI Magazine*, *27*(4), pp. 12–12.

McLuhan, M. 1964. *Understanding Media: The Extensions of Man*. London: Routledge.

Müller, V.C. ed. 2016. *Risks of Artificial Intelligence*. London: CRC Press.

Newman, C. 2017. The wisdom of trees: they inspire us, comfort us, and remind us how life moves on. *National Geographic*, *231*(3), p. 52.

Noble, D. 1984. *Forces of Production: A Social History of Industrial Automation*. London: Routledge.

OECD. 2019a. What are the OECD Principles on AI? Last accessed in June, 2020: www.oecd.org/going-digital/ai/principles/

OECD. 2019b. Artificial Intelligence in Society. Last accessed in June, 2020. www.legalinstruments.oecd.org/en/instruments/OECD-LEGAL-0449

Petropoulos, G. 2018. The impact of artificial intelligence on employment. *Praise for Work in the Digital Age*, p. 119.

Reuters. 2018. Amazon scraps secret AI recruiting tool that showed bias against women. Last accessed in June, 2020: www.reuters.com/article/us-amazon-com-jobs-automation-insight/amazon-scraps-secret-ai-recruiting-tool-that-showed-bias-against-women-idUSKCN1MK08G

RIAA. 2019. *2019 RIAA Shipment and Revenue*. Last accessed in June 2020: www.riaa.com/u-s-sales-database/

Sato, T. 2011. Representation of desire and femininity. In I. Lassen, ed., *Living with Patriarchy: Discursive Constructions of Gendered Subjects Across Cultures* (Vol. 45). Amsterdam, The Netherlands: John Benjamins Publishing. pp. 145–166.

Sato, T. 2013. Ethics and responsibility in international business. In D. Tsang, H.H. Kazeroony, and G. Ellis, eds., *The Routledge Companion to International Management Education*. London: Routledge. pp. 86–103.

Sato, T. 2014. Creative destruction and music streaming in the age of diversity. *Valerij Dermol Anna Rakowska. The Age of Diversity*. Lublin, Poland. pp. 53–70.

Schumpeter, J. 1942. Creative destruction. *Capitalism, Socialism and Democracy*, *825*, pp. 82–85.

Tackney, C. T. 2018. Authenticity in employment relations: A theology of the workplace analysis. *Journal of Management, Spirituality & Religion*, *15*(1), pp. 82–104.

Turing, A. 1950. Computing intelligence and machinery. *Mind*, *59*(2236), pp. 433–460.

Veblen, T., 1899/1934. *The Theory of the Leisure Class: An Economic Study of Institutions*. New York: The Macmillan Company.

VF Magazine. 2016. *Could These New Pressing Machines Save the Record Industry?* Last accessed in July 2020: www.thevinylfactory.com/features/could-these-new-pressing-machines-save-the-record-industry/

Walsh, W. 2020. *AI 'Outperforms' Doctors Diagnosing Breast Cancer*. Last accessed in July 2020: www.bbc.com/news/health-50857759

Winner, L. 1993. Upon opening the black box and finding it empty: Social constructivism and the philosophy of technology. *Science, Technology, & Human Values*, *18*(3), pp. 362–378.

Yudkowsky, E. 2008. Artificial intelligence as a positive and negative factor in global risk. *Global Catastrophic Risks*, *1*(303), p. 184.

Part II

Future of Work and Leadership

Generational and Skill Gap

5 Workplace Learning and Generation Z

Technology-led Learning

Guy Ellis

Introduction

Generation Z, or GenZ, were born between 1995 and 2015 and are the newest generation to enter the world of work. GenZ is so new to the workforce that there has not been a lot of peer-reviewed research on them, and what is available has been primarily based on a formal educational setting. However, less methodically robust research has been emerging over the last few years from large consultancies and service providers. While we need to treat such data with caution, trends begin to paint a picture of a generation that learns – and believes in the importance of learning – very differently from previous cohorts. GenZ is often called digital natives, with its 8-second attention span, constant use of smartphones, addiction to watching videos, and demands for work--life balance. One would have thought they would be the vanguard of artificial intelligence (AI) learning. But the picture seems to be far more nuanced than that. This generation also demands face time (as opposed to FaceTime), prioritizes human interaction, and wants highly engaged managers to give them regular, frequent feedback.

While they have a desire for constant development, it needs to be within an organizational purpose. GenZ has the skills to make snap judgments about online content and deep dive into the data to find out more. They need personalized experiences but want to work in a positive team environment. GenZ wants a blend of high touch with high tech, AI with a human interface. This chapter covers the latest thinking and research on how GenZ learns in the workplace and what this means for technology learning, AI, and International Management Education (IME) going forward.

Who Is GenZ?

While there is some disagreement about the specific start and end dates, the consensus is that GenZ covers people born between 1995 and 2015 (Scott & Ellis, 2020).

There are perennial arguments about the value of labeling any group of individuals based on the years they were born and the drivers that shaped them. Underpinned by the global and pervasive reach of the internet, and social media, suggest that the five generations labeled from the Silent Generation of 1925 to 1945 have the most reasons to show similar characteristics. The lexicon of different generations has also entered common usage – Millennials (Generation Y), Gen X, and Baby Boomers and Silent Generation. Researchers, politicians, and business people have used the terms and the general population to attribute positive and negative labels and refine their broader messages.

The arbitrary allocation of birth dates defines each generation, and the length of each generation varies between 15 and 20 years. Each generation is shaped by the societal, economic, and lately, technological forces that impacted it. For example, it was the population explosion and economic expansion for Baby Boomers following World War II. For GenZ, the global financial crisis of 2008 was one of the most significant forces (Network for Executive Women & Deloitte, 2018). At an impressionable age – the earliest GenZer was 13 – the crisis and subsequent years saw millions losing their jobs and livelihoods, homes, and entire way of life. The preteenagers watched it happening and then felt the consequences personally. And they saw the senior managers of those companies which caused the crash not be held accountable for their actions.

Although September 11 happened when most were too young to remember, the second primary driver that defines GenZ has been the terrorism and random violence that followed. From indiscriminate attacks across the globe justified by religious dogma and extremist ideology, the significant upsurge in school shootings in the USA and elsewhere, major wars in the Middle East, and numerous minor ones, this generation has witnessed firsthand, thanks to the internet, brutality rarely seen since World War II. The next primary driver is the emergence into mainstream society of climate change. In contrast, a topic of concern and interest to various groups for over 50 years, the continued rise of greenhouse gases and failure at an international level to agree and implement modest actions to reduce them gave rise to a global movement calling on measures to be taken. Fronted by well-known GenZers, the campaign has resonated with many of their generations as they perceive that a lack of global action has put their long-term future on the planet at risk. While we are unsure if this coming-of-age issue for GenZ could encapsulate their distinct character, there is no doubt that, for many GenZers, they will be the generation that stops talking and starts acting.

The rise of the internet has been both a primary driver and enabler for GenZ. The first generation to have internet access literally since birth has bought both good and bad but is a core part of their daily life, every bit as much as electricity is to GenX. As a driver, it allowed them to reach out to people worldwide for friendships not based on locality or their senses but shared interests. But it also bombarded them with data, fake news, and the ability to comment on any aspect of others' life anonymously. As an enabler, it brought far-flung violence and bad news and customized marketing based on their preferences. It also gave them razor-like skills to distinguish between data, information, and knowledge. Technology is the final key driver for this generation. The Millennials were bought up on technology; GenZ has experienced rapid broadband speed, handheld hardware that is more powerful than previous mainframes, and untold numbers of applications (apps) that allow them to personalize their experiences with the outside world.

As I write this chapter, the Covid-19 (Corona) virus is sweeping the world. The response from national and international authorities is unprecedented in terms of the role that government is currently playing in the populace's ordinary lives. Everyday life has been suspended, with severe restrictions on daily activities and citizen movement across the globe. While it is far too early to tell what the impact might be on GenZ, there is every chance that this global event may yet come to define this generation more than the Financial Crash of 2008, the rise of terrorism, the mainstreaming of climate change, the internet and technology.

Given these drivers, is it surprising that GenerationZ looks for security and certainty in a demonstrably unstable world? That they are determined to right wrongs that they saw as youngsters? That they think life without a broader purpose can bring misery to millions? Is that technology their gateway to the world?

GenZ and Their Approach to Technology

GenZ lives and breathes technology and the internet. GenZ is the first generation to experience the internet since birth. Google was founded when the oldest was only three years old. The mainstream USA adopted the internet at the turn of the century (Wikipedia contributors, 2020) – and as digital natives, GenZ is always wedded to its internet devices, typically mobiles, for up to ten hours (Desjardins, 2019) a day. Research reinforces the famous digital natives' label.

GenZ has the shortest attention span of all the generations – 8 seconds compared to Millennials' 12 – but that's when providers of content have to get their attention (Workforce Institute at Kronos, 2019). If a GenZer sees something that looks interesting, they can engage for hours over multiple channels to truly understand the topic. GenZ can also scan and move between five screens at once compared to the Millennials three. This generation also seems to be capable of doing this repeatedly without any significant loss of focus elsewhere, i.e., switching tasks at a rapid rate with no significant drop-off in concentration.

But this skill comes with an expectation of consumer-grade technology and connection levels with the internet. If connections are too slow or the app is chunky or not user-friendly, GenZ will move on mostly on mobile.

GenZ will instinctively go online for visual learning before thinking about reading or asking about it. Education is also about interacting rather than merely consuming. For this cohort, YouTube is the most recognized content provider. The British Ofcom media regulator's report for 2019 (Ofcom, 2019) highlights that young people are merely abandoning traditional television and television news. In contrast, Baby Boomers (1946–1965) watch over half an hour of television news a day, GenZ watch two minutes.

With regard to social media and apps, GenZ's favorite social media is YouTube, and, in UK research, more GenZers recognized YouTube compared to the BBC (94% vs. 82%) (Ofcom, 2020). Partly this is because YouTube provides a multisensory experience, i.e., text, visual, and auditory, and because GenZ want to interact with their learning, share it, and comment.

However, GenZ will have multiple social media accounts, have different personas on each one, and use them for various purposes. Social media and apps also need to be personalized to them, and their need to offer two-way communication and learn from their usage. There are hundreds of social media platforms and millions of apps – if one doesn't meet their needs or another provider offers a better experience, GenZ will move on.

Finally, GenZ is also into gaming in multiple formats – first-person adventure/shooter game or puzzle app played as an individual or online multiplayer, classic, or card games. However, this multibillion-dollar industry often provides insight into what future learning technology and apps might look like and teaches educators how and why young people use such programs. Games can be a distraction from real life, but they also provide the user with immediate feedback, a multisensory experience, and reinforce the importance of learning from your mistakes. Technology and the internet are the lifeblood of GenZ and need to create effective organizational workplace learning.

GenZ and Learning

The societal events that shaped GenZ have had a significant impact on their willingness to learn and how they do so. GenZ is an avid learner. They crave long-term financial security, but they also understand the importance of learning new skills and continuously developing themselves (INSEAD 2017) while they want a good salary in the short term. Learning provides GenZ with the skills and knowledge to be more successful in their current role and increase their choices for developing or even switching careers in the longer term. GenZ does not want to end up in a dead-end job or careers like their older cousins, the Millennials, or parents.

Unlike previous generations, GenZ takes responsibility for their learning (IBM Corporation, 2017), although, in part, this is now much easier with the plethora of self-help videos available on social media. This generation is often described as pragmatic self-starters who know that life is not sanitized or perfect. They need to take personal responsibility and the initiative to get things done. This uniqueness also makes teaching GenZ a different prospect to other generations. GenZ also wants purpose. They want to feel as though they are making a difference, that their actions will help others, and is linked to a long-term objective. This desire shapes what GenZ are willing to learn and, unless they can see a benefit, with or without the help of their organization, they will not put the energy into absorbing the information.

Technology is a critical tool for this generation when it comes to learning. As previously noted, GenZ are true digital natives, and their internet-connected devices are to them what electricity is to GenX; they could not imagine life without it. As practical go-getters, GenZ have learned and taught both directly and formally all of their life that the information they want is available online and typically can be viewed as a video. Also, gaming apps have taught GenZ a much more relaxed attitude to failure because losing a 'life' is no big deal and means receiving immediate feedback on both what works and what doesn't (Scott & Ellis, 2020).

One significant consequence of on-demand technology, short attention spans, and personalized apps is that GenZ seek experiences. While many researchers have made the point that using a multimedia and sensory approach to engage with GenZ, they have missed that this generation does not see learning as a separate exercise from the rest of their work–life in the learning context. Training and development are an integral part of work, from the minute that they thought about applying for a role to have well left the organization. It also means that they want appropriate training when they need it, i.e., on-demand, and that training and development is a mix of formal and informal, classroom and on-the-job, technology, and coaching.

It would seem at this point that all the existing research is leading to a potential explosion of technology-led learning as GenZ enter the workforce and become the largest working generation by 2030. However, despite their noticeable comfort with technology and social media, two major factors will hold back the introduction of technology-led learning for GenZ. The first factor is that GenZ value the advice and information from their friends and family above all other sources. Although seemingly a contradiction to their social media reliance, for GenZ, this is all about trust. In other words, while they love the delivery mechanism, GenZ is skeptical of the content. The Noughties' financial crisis and the ongoing climate change debate have led GenZ to be cynical of what organizations and authority figures say. To them, machine-led learning potentially represents an idealized version of corporate-speak that is neither practical nor reflective of how organizations operate. What this means in practice for education is that while GenZ will continue to seek out and absorb computer-based information, they will want confirmation and context for that learning from people that they trust – friends, family, their manager, and peers. Research also strongly suggests that the manager's role is critical for GenZ (Workforce Institute at Kronos, 2019). They expect their managers to be credible, trustworthy, and want them to provide regular feedback in a mentoring style. For GenZ, managers and leaders provide context, a dose of reality, and enable learning to be personalized for their specific circumstances and needs.

The second factor is their learning experiences to date, primarily learning institutions such as schools, colleges, and universities. It is impossible to accurately capture all of the global nuances of how GenZ is formally taught. However, the traditional classroom model-based learning with a teacher/lecturer/professor at the front talking to their students and providing them with all of the information they need to know is a myth. While varying from country to country, the education sector has internationally recognized the many weaknesses of such a single approach. Instead, GenZ's formal schooling can be broadly characterized by a mix of traditional classroom teaching, self-learning, group-based work, and community endeavors, assessed by rigorous standard examinations and a range of more or less structured assessments including coursework, presentations, and team-based exercises. Critically, while technology plays a role in formal learning, formal educational institutions recognize that it is only one aspect of a multidimensional approach. Organizations that want to educate GenZers in IME, or any other training and development, need to use technology. But for learning to be effective, they need to integrate that technology with a human touch.

GenZ Difference: Integrating Human Touch and Technology

Organizations are frequently criticized for their approach to learning and development. While this chapter is not the place to examine that debate, a recent Harvard Business Review article (Glaveski, 2019) highlighted the key issues – the wrong training and development delivered at the wrong time, which is quickly forgotten. GenZ accentuates such problems with their short attention spans, expectations of on-demand information, ability to see through irrelevance, and willingness to question accepted orthodoxies. If organizations want to train and develop their GenZ employees effectively, they will have to rethink their traditional workplace learning approach. The key aspects that organizations will need to consider are (Scott & Ellis, 2020):

- The technology platform – learning will need to be accessible anytime, anyplace, and be underpinned by consumer-grade technology
- Create learning experiences, coordinated and delivered across the entire employee life cycle
- Learning provided across multiple learning channels
- The context provided by managers links learning to clear employee and organizational needs.

The great news is that unlike previous generations, GenZ will take responsibility for their learning. Provided organizations can provide context, tools, and information, GenZ will perceive education as a practical benefit and not a chore or theoretical resource. Technology is the platform from which learning commences for GenZ (Hays, 2019). While friends and family are critical, technology sources and social media are the starting point for forming initial thoughts and observations to discuss and debate. However, technology needs to be consumer-grade, i.e., fast and readily available with minimal access processes. Many organizations will struggle to deliver using large, server-based human resources systems. The technology also requires integration, so the information is captured in one app shared with all others, e.g., completed learning is captured in both the learning management system and performance management system.

GenZ embrace experiences (The Deloitte Global Millennial Survey, 2019), events that connect multisensory learning with a purpose. This is encapsulated by their passion for the social media platform YouTube video content and abundance of do-it-yourself how-to content. Organizations can embrace this approach by using multiple learning channels and using a model such as an employee life cycle that captures the entire employee workplace experience and creates a story for learners. The employee life cycle starts with the *recruitment* process as potential candidates become employees, their initial *onboarding* entry into the organization, their ongoing *training and development, management of their performance, rewarding and recognizing* their contribution, and concluding when the employee *exits* the organization. Technology can be a crucial foundation for creating an integrated employee experience across the GenZ life cycle.

To meet GenZers' short attention span, practical nature, desire not to label themselves, and wish to own their learning, organizations need to recognize the importance of just-in-time delivery, microlearning, and offering multiple learning channels. For GenZ, there is no one ideal approach to learning, no one right time to learn, and while they prefer to learn skills just before they need them, they want to be given the responsibility for making their own choices. Organizations can meet this need by offering a range of learning platforms – video, written, verbal – either via technology or face to face, but need to recognize that GenZ also need clear guidance and appropriate tools.

The final element is context and purpose (INSEAD 2017). GenZ are a pragmatic generation who desire a purpose. While they value learning, they will not be prepared to commit energy to it without understanding why it's important and how it will make a difference and what is required by them. However, the purpose is pragmatic and can be short term, e.g., how do I write a business plan, or longer term, e.g., how can I learn project management skills. While formal documents such as mission and value statements provide some context, through the performance management process and daily management of GenZ by their managers, they will relate their role, learning needs, and opportunities to the organization's greater needs. This guidance can come through clear policies and tools such as career ladders, personal guidance through mechanisms such as mentoring and coaching programs, or through the formal and informal performance management process and day-to-day management from their managers. In summary, while technology, learning experiences, and multiple learning channels are critical to effective GenZ learning, managers and learning professionals' context and purpose is the glue that holds it all together.

Work Practice: GenZ Employee Life Cycle

What might effective and efficient learning look like at the organizational level? The following is how an organization might approach GenZ learning, using the employee life cycle model to maximize its impact. For GenZ, training and development starts even before they apply for a role. Typically, if interested in working for an organization, a GenZer will extensively research the organization, both online and via friends and family, to find out all they can (LinkedIn, 2020). The GenZ research is a chance for organizations to help GenZ candidates learn about the development opportunities, highlight critical policies such as diversity and equality, time-off and corporate social responsibility, and to demonstrate through practical examples of what life is really like when working for the organization (Monster Worldwide, 2016). Using real stories of current GenZ employees who tell it like it is positive and negative is a powerful influencing tool for this generation (Millennial Branding & Ranstad, 2014).

Onboarding, the first few weeks and months of a new employee's work life, is a critical time for organizations to maximize ongoing employee engagement (Hirsch, 2017). For a new GenZ employee, time to reinforce what it learned about the organization through the recruitment process, begin the learning process, and the technology will support them, receiving clear expectations about the development going forward and understand the mechanisms for providing context to that learning. Onboarding also extends the recruitment experience into the working environment. Examples of such education might include allowing GenZers to access high-quality early-day training such as health and safety, providing them with microprojects to understand how the organization works, and early access to critical decision-makers.

The training and development stage of the employee life cycle continues the processes started in recruitment and induction. Organizations must provide a range of methods for GenZ to learn, such as an online learning management system and face to face to include formal mentoring and coaching program, classroom, and on-the-job training. GenZ will appreciate other ways to learn and develop, such as being part of a project team, secondments, and opportunities to meet up with colleagues outside of their normal work processes (Upwork, 2019). Wherever possible, training needs to be linked to either the GenZ's specific role or potential future opportunities. As mentioned, online training and development need to be accessible anytime and anywhere, i.e., outside of the work environment and personal devices. Organizations can also significantly benefit from educating line and senior managers about the unique aspects of GenZ with practical examples and skills on how to manage and motivate them.

Performance management is where training and development meet the reality of the work environment and the everyday activities of the GenZ employee. The organization, typically through the GenZers' manager, provides a critical context for why learning is essential and how it can be applied (The Centre for Generational Kinetics, LLC, 2018). Feedback is the lifeblood of GenZers and allows GenZ to learn from their failures and make their way around what, for many of them, is initially an unfamiliar and ambiguous environment (McKinsey and Company, 2017). Technology also has a vital role in supporting managers to link the GenZers' learning with the organization's broader goals and purpose. Also, it allows the organization to offer a more nuanced and flexible approach to GenZ learning needs than the traditional annual model. Learning can be a sufficient reward and recognition tool for GenZ. Provided such learning is personalized education that offers both the organization and GenZ employees immediate and long-term benefits.

Finally, the exit process allows the organization to teach the GenZ employee that while the next stage of their career may not be with them, their future experiences might be welcomed back for both parties' benefit. Viewing organizational learning across the employee life cycle helps organizations coordinate all aspects of GenZ learning and recognizes that this generation sees learning as an integrated process tied to specific short- and long-term needs.

Conclusion

GenZ represents organizations' opportunity to truly integrate technology-led training and development into the workplace learning paradigm. Technology-led training has stumbled toward making a significant impact because it typically stands alone from more traditional delivery models with little context as to its application. However, it is a feature of workplace learning for over 30 years, loved by finance for its low cost and human resources for its reach. Organizations who want to engage with GenZ, with their desire to learn, willingness to take responsibility for their development, and no-nonsense, tell it like it is an approach to life; need to rethink their whole learning approach.

Organizations need to create a collective learning experience, built on a suitable technology platform, using multiple delivery channels with context and links to organizational and personal needs. Fundamentally, this learning paradigm needs to be actively supported by management. Without this human touch, GenZ will seek validation from colleagues and others outside their organization, undermining key messages and application.

Covid-19 (Coronavirus) Update

As mentioned earlier in the chapter, Covid-19 is sweeping the planet with unprecedented consequences to global health and economic well-being. While the pandemic effects will continue to be felt for years to come, it is too early to assess how, if at all, the world of work will change. However, some of the most noticeable effects of the global lockdown have been the change to working patterns and the rise of working from home, the proliferation of video conferencing use, and online learning. This pandemic has been an opportunity for technology-led education to demonstrate how powerful and effective this delivery mechanism can be. However, from a well-being perspective, Covid-19 has already had a more significant mental health impact (but lower physical impact) on GenZ compared to any other generation – further proof that this generation needs a human touch.

References

Desjardins, J. (2019). *Meet Generation Z: The Newest Member to the Workforce*. Visual Capitalist. February 14. www.visualcapitalist.com/meet-generation-z-the-newest-member-to-the-workforce/

Glaveski, S. (2019). *Where Companies Go Wrong with Learning and Development*. Harvard Business Publishing. October 2. https://hbr.org/2019/10/where-companies-go-wrong-with-learning-and-development

Hays (2019). *What Workers Want Report: Mindset Key for Digital Change*. www.hays.co.uk/what-workers-want

Hirsch, A.S. (2017). *Don't Underestimate the Importance of Good Onboarding*. Society for Human Resource Management (SHRM). August 10. www.shrm.org/resourcesandtools/hr-topics/talent-acquisition/pages/dont-underestimate-the-importance-of-effective-onboarding.aspx

IBM Corporation (2017). *Uniquely Generation Z: What Brands Should Know about Today's Youngest Consumers*. www.ibm.com/thought-leadership/institute-business-value/report/uniquelygenz

INSEAD (2017). *Brave New Workplace: A Look at How Generations X, Y and Z Are Reshaping the Nature of Work*. INSEAD, Universum, The HEAD Foundation and MIT Leadership Centre. www.insead.edu/news/2017-brave-new-workplace-with-gen-xyz

LinkedIn (2020). *2020 Global Talent Trends: 4 Trends Changing the Way You Attract and Retain Talent*. https://business.linkedin.com/talent-solutions/blog/trends-and-research/2020/global-talent-trends-2020

McKinsey and Company (2017). *'True Gen': Generation Z and Its Implications for Companies*. www.mckinsey.com/industries/consumer-packaged-goods/our-insights/true-gen-generation-z-and-its-implications-for-companies

Millennial Branding & Randstad (2014). *Gen Y and Gen Z Global Workplace Expectations Study.* http://millennialbranding.com/2014/geny-genz-global-workplace-expectations-study/

Monster Worldwide (2016). *Move Over, Millennials: What You'll Need to Know for Hiring as Gen Z Enters the Workforce.* https://hiring.monster.com/litereg/genzreport.aspx

Network for Executive Women & Deloitte (2018). *Welcome to Generation Z.* www2.deloitte.com/content/dam/Deloitte/us/Documents/consumer-business/welcome-to-gen-z.pdf

Ofcom (2019). *Communications Market Report 2019 – Interactive Data.* www.ofcom.org.uk/research-and-data/multi-sector-research/cmr/cmr-2019/interactive

Ofcom (2020). *An Exploration of People's Relationship with PSB, with a Particular Focus on the Views of Young People – Qualitative Research Report.* July. www.ofcom.org.uk/__data/assets/pdf_file/0024/199104/exploration-of-peoples-relationship-with-psb.pdf

Scott, G. & Ellis, G. (2020). *GenZ Insight: How to Make Your Organisation a GenZ Magnet.* The Message Medium: On demand.

The Centre for Generational Kinetics, LLC (2018). *The State of Gen Z 2018: Unexpected Insights into How Gen Z Is Impacting Everything from Technology and Brands to Social Media and the Workplace.* https://genhq.com/generation-z-research-2018/

The Deloitte Global Millennial Survey (2019). *Societal Discord and Technological Transformation Create a "Generation Disrupted".* www2.deloitte.com/global/en/pages/about-deloitte/articles/millennialsurvey.html

Upwork (2019). *Future Workforce 2019: How Younger Generations Are Reshaping the Future Workforce.* www.upwork.com/press/2019/03/05/third-annual-future-workforce-report/

Wikipedia contributors (2020). *History of the Internet.* Wikipedia, The Free Encyclopedia. April 3, 21:41 UTC. https://en.wikipedia.org/w/index.php?title=History_of_the_Internet&oldid=948947211

Workforce Institute at Kronos (2019). *Full Report: Generation Z in the Workplace.* https://workforceinstitute.org/wp-content/uploads/2019/11/Full-Report-Generation-Z-in-the-Workplace.pdf

6 Industry 4.0 and its Impact on Future Business Leaders

Aneta Aleksander

Introduction

The fourth industrial revolution (Industry 4.0) constitutes a conceptual aggregate covering several new technologies – including the Internet of Things, cloud computing, big data analysis, artificial intelligence, and incremental printing, augmented reality, and collaborative robots. Another dimension of Industry 4.0 is related to production management, an enterprise's organization, and creating a value chain. In particular, the architecture of production management systems is changing. The transition from linear processes and the traditional pyramid of production management systems to the network of connections and nonlinear production can be observed. The combination of the previously mentioned innovations with new possibilities in artificial intelligence may, in effect, lead to a revolutionary change in production management methods, where the systems will operate in a highly autonomous manner, dynamically changing their structure and functions within the organization.

These ongoing changes will require a new approach to management and leadership. On the one hand, they will force managers and leaders to develop technical and engineering competences continually. At the same time, on the other, they will require the development of new social competences and a new leadership model. Remote work projects implemented and realized in virtual and multicultural teams are already becoming the norm. Moreover, the pandemic situation that the world has faced from the 2019 year even strengthened and accelerated these processes, causing employees, team members, managers, and leaders to adapt to new conditions quickly. The remote work in virtual teams and the use of all ICT solutions became an everyday reality, not just a theory widely described in the literature and used sporadically in extraordinary situations. In this regard, we can say that the future came earlier than one could expect. In these circumstances, the traditional approach to human resource management may not be enough. Therefore, I will outline new challenges for leadership and leaders in the era of Industry 4.0.

This chapter in the theoretical part will contain a review of the literature on Industry 4.0 and leadership competences that will be necessary for skillful leading and managing in the era of Industry 4.0. The empirical part will be based on research conducted with a sample of 553 enterprises from the small- and medium-sized enterprises (SME) sector in Poland. The study focused on the current state of the Industry's 4.0 elements and SME's sector companies and their leaders' readiness to implement Industry 4.0 solutions. The research was conducted from December 2019 to March 2020.

The Traditional Approach to Leadership

Leadership is currently widely described in the literature of management sciences, and the idea of leadership seems to be gaining in importance. However, it was not always so. In the 1950s, research was primarily conducted on organization and management, such as the well-known book "Organizations" by March and Simon (1958). The term leadership appeared neither in the table of contents nor in the subject index (Kuc, 2004, p. 375). At that time, leadership was associated with a formal position. All forms of individual acts of leadership were treated as voluntary actions, or in the negative sense of the word – as insubordination (Kuc, 2004, p. 374). However, since the 1930s, leadership has been studied in the USA, how people became leaders, what determined their effectiveness, and how the term was applied in formal organizations and groups (Kuc, 2004, p. 375).

There are many definitions of leadership in scientific literature. Maxwell (2001) explained leadership is *influencing*. Robbins (1998) described it as the ability to *influence the group to achieve specific goals*. Terry (1997) expounded leadership as the act of *influencing people so that they are willing to pursue group goals*. Leadership is the *process of influencing others to achieve certain goals in certain situations without using coercion* (Williams, DuBrin, & Sisk, 1985). Rutka (2001 pointed out that *leadership consists of an emotional state, prompting followers to commit to organizational goals based on their actions*. Leadership is an *increase in the influence that exceeds the mechanical adjustment to the organization's routinized demands* (Katz & Kahn, 1979, pp. 464–466). Leadership occurs when a goal requires many to simultaneously achieve it (Armstrong, 1999, pp. 225–226).

Leadership is about encouraging and inspiring individuals and teams to do their best to achieve the desired result. Leadership is both a process and a property (Stogdill, 1974). The leadership process is the unforced direction and coordination of members of an organized group to achieve group goals. As a property, leadership is a set of personality traits attributed to those perceived to be using it successfully. These traits must differentiate leaders significantly. A similar definition of leadership was adopted by Griffin (2004), according to which leadership involves the use of influence, without resorting to coercive measures, to shape the goals of a group or organization, motivating behaviors aimed at achieving these goals and helping to define a culture of a group or organization.

De Pree (1999) argued that the driving force for employees is not the loud voice of the leader, the whip's shooting, or his or her television personality. De Pree (1999) thought leadership gave people a chance to achieve what is asked of them most humanely and effectively. Thus, the leader is like a *servant* to followers as they remove obstacles that prevent them from carrying out their duties. In short, true leaders enable their followers to use all their opportunities. A leader must be able to think clearly to be effective. Leaders must, therefore, be clear about their views. Leaders need to carefully consider their assumptions about human nature, the organization's role, work efficiency measures, and many other issues. De Pree (1999) defined leadership as the art of *mastery, tribal than scientific character, the interweaving of interpersonal relationships*. De Pree argued that leadership is not the quality of the mind but the attitude toward others. The art of leadership requires that we treat the leader as the host in terms of interpersonal relationships. Burns (1978) pointed out the role of values in the leadership as the process and the leadership as properties that characterize the leader. He claimed that a leader who omits the moral components of leadership might go down in history as a scoundrel, or even worse. Moral leadership is about values and requires providing team members with enough information about the different options for action to make a wise choice when responding to the leader's suggestions.

The common feature of all definitions of leadership is the emphasis on *influencing others*, bearing in mind the compromise of three elements: character traits, specific behaviors, and situations. All these occur depending on the needs of the moment. Leadership researchers see a potential leader as exceptional, unique, endowed with a great and strong personality, which attracts others to themselves by their individual behavior, not only by their position. Leaders use power to build, not ruin a group, which can effectively use different styles to influence their followers (Kuc, 2004).

Some scholars argued that leaders are born (Stodgill, 1974; Katz & Kahn, 1979; Aronson, Wilson, & Akert, 1997; Kouzes & Posner, 2003). Other scholars argued that leadership qualities and leadership skills could be developed and acquired with experience (Drucker, 1976; Stoner, Freeman, & Gilbert Jr., 1999; Armstrong, 1999). Drucker (1976) penned, if leaders were born, why many books are written about being a leader. Drucker continued that the diversity in the group of influential leaders is so great that it is difficult to say anything meaningful about their character and temperament's common properties. According to Drucker (2000), leadership is *acting with a sense of responsibility*. It is important to have followers and to set a good example yourself. In a similar vein, Stoner et al. (1999) expressed that based on the research, there are no features that clearly and consistently distinguish leaders from non-leaders. Leaders as a community are indeed more clever, extroverted, and self-confident than non-leaders. Yet millions of people share the same qualities and will never become leaders. Therefore, it is difficult to state unequivocally whether leaders' specific characteristics are the cause of leadership abilities or the result of the leadership experience related to their leadership position (Stoner et al. 1999; Kuc, 2004).

There are people whose inborn personality traits predispose them to perform leadership activities more than others, and there are those who, even by learning to manage, do not have a chance of becoming good leaders (Zieleniewski, 1976). But both can benefit from learning to lead. The talented can develop their talent; lacking talent – partially replace it with the acquired skill.

Leadership, both as a process and as a property, can take various forms, which is mainly determined by three elements (Tannenbaum & Schmidt, 1958):

1   the person of the leader – along with his or her knowledge, skills and abilities, competences, personality traits, sensitivity to the situational factors;
2   situation in which leadership phenomena take place – time constraints, type of problem, required information and knowledge, organization characteristics – traditions and values, size and location, safety requirements;
3   the team and its members – their knowledge, competences, ambitions, motivation, and attitude. The need for independence, tolerance of ambiguity, identification with the goals of the organization.

With the above determinants in mind, the leadership researchers distinguished several types and styles of leadership and related categories of leaders. Among them are charismatic and nonismatic, autocratic and democratic, visionary and controller, transactional and transformational, narcissistic, possessive, seductive, and prudent (Strategor, 1999). The leadership styles presented in the literature on the subject are shown in Table 6.1.

Regardless of the inborn traits, knowledge, and skills, but depending on the correlation of the right features at the right time, a detailed list of factors influencing success can be distinguished (Armstrong, 1999). There are among others the following:

•   the ability to work with people
•   the ability to take responsibility for the main tasks
•   the need to achieve results
•   leadership experience in the early stages of career
•   wide range of experiences
•   ability to make deals and negotiate
•   willingness to take risks

Table 6.1 Leadership styles

Style of leadership	Leader's behavior	The essence of style	Underlying emotional intelligence competencies	Optimal results	Overall impact on the working atmosphere
Coercive	Demands immediate compliance.	"Do what I tell you."	Focus on achievement, initiative, self-control.	In a crisis (in order to quickly start a restructuring program) or in dealing with difficult employees.	Negative
Authoritative	Mobilizes people to implement a shared vision.	"Come with me."	Self-confidence, empathy, catalyzing change.	When a change requires a new vision or when a clear course of action is needed.	Usually positive
Affiliative	Cares for harmonious human relations and creates emotional bonds.	"People come first."	Empathy, relationship building, communication.	When you need to overcome divisions in the team or motivate discouraged employees.	Positive
Democratic	Forges consensus through participation.	"What do you think?"	Collaboration, team leadership, communication.	When it comes to gaining support, building consensus, or gaining valuable employees for cooperation.	Positive
Pacesetting	Sets high criteria for the quality of work.	"Do as I do, now."	Conscientiousness, achievement-oriented, initiative.	When it is necessary to achieve quick results with a team of motivated and competent employees.	Negative
Coaching	Develops other people in terms of their professional perspectives.	"Try this."	Developing others, empathy, self-awareness.	If it is necessary to help an employee improve the effects of work or develop their lasting advantages.	Positive

Source: Author's own study on the basis of D. Goleman (2000), Leadership That Gets Results, *Harvard Business Review*, *HBR OnPoint*, Available on-line 20.03.2020: https://intranet.ecu.edu.au/__data/assets/pdf_file/0011/773867/HBR-Leadership-thar-gets-results-by-D-Gole_-.pdf

- the ability to have better ideas than colleagues
- help from immediate superiors in developing talents
- the ability to adapt the management style to the current situation

Leadership is one of the essential elements of the management process. It is directly related to the organization's human factor, which, despite four industrial revolutions that have been identified as milestones in the evolution of technology, is still a vital element of any organization. What is necessarily associated with a human being are emotions, motivations, and relationships, and as A. Blikle (2014) writes, leadership is precisely the ability to shape emotions and relationships (Blikle, 2014, p. 92). Hence, the rest of this chapter will deal with new challenges faced by leaders in the era of constant technical and technological changes and changing social conditions.

Industry 4.0 Leaders' Competences and Traits

Contemporary reality creates new conditions and new paths of leadership development. We are witnessing many changes that take place not only in the area of technology, production, and manufacturing methods, digitization of industrial processes, but also changes in social areas related to people, changes in the system of values and beliefs, generational differences. Thus they cause a shift in life approach, the desire to maintain a balance between personal and professional life (life–work balance). The economy in which we currently operate is the so-called knowledge-based economy, which in turn entails, on the one hand, benefits in the form of the desire for continuous improvement and the possibility of the constant development of technical competences. On the other hand, it is associated with developing social competences, greater awareness of employees, increasing the level of requirements, and increasing independence. Therefore, leadership creates the need to acquire unique technical and psychosocial skills understanding the expectations and the proper use of their knowledge, skills, and talents (Stachowicz-Stanusch & Aleksander, 2018).

The challenge is also to build effective teams of people who will see a sense in working together, whose individual skills and knowledge, when combined, will create a synergy effect conducive to the effective achievement of the organization's goals. Blikle (2014) argued that as physics laws, there are forcefields that make some people attract each other and others repel, which is crucial in building a harmonious team fulfilling members' ambitions with dignity, addressing spiritual needs. As the Centre for Executive Education stated,

> more than ever, leaders have to navigate unfamiliar, challenging times, a quickening pace of change, increasing expectations, and a rising tide of rapidly evolving conditions. This new and different environment is

challenging leaders to find new ways to lead their organizations and achieve sustained success. Because of these circumstances, there is a thirst for leadership, yet leaders face a whirlwind environment laden with remarkable opportunities and daunting challenges through which to lead their people and organizations.

(Centre for Executive Education, 2018)

The Industry 4.0 promotes the manufacturing industry's automation, creating so-called smart-automated and robotized factories, mass-indi-vidualization of production and products, and a high level of customiza-tion based on user experience (ASTOR, 2018). Industry 4.0 encompasses the following key technologies: cloud computing, industrial Internet of Things, cybersecurity, integration of systems, incremental manufac-turing, big data, augmented and virtual reality, smart automation and robotics, simulations (ASTOR, 2018). In short, the idea of Industry 4.0 means that smart factories in which machines are augmented with web connectivity and connected to a system that can visualize the entire pro-duction chain and make decisions on its own. In this fourth revolution, many new technologies will evolve that combine the physical, digital, and biological worlds.

The new technologies will impact all disciplines, economies, and industries, and even challenge our ideas about what it means to be human (Bawany, 2019). As Bawany (2018a) claimed, we live today in a highly disruptive and increasingly VUCA-driven world (volatile, uncer-tain, complex, and ambiguous), becoming much more challenging. In recent times, the explosion of data and unprecedented advances in com-puter processing power globally have dramatically increased the cap-acity to support decision-making within various functional operations in organizations across industries. The impact of advanced technologies touches virtually every industry and organization on many levels, from strategic planning and marketing to supply chain management and cus-tomer service (Bawany, 2018b). There are many famous examples of companies that have transformed our lifestyles, including how we travel, shop, and stay. One can mention such companies as Uber, Alibaba, Airbnb, Netflix, and Tesla, and many more (Bawany, 2018a). The current conditions require understanding the next generation (NextGen) of leaders who must acquire cognitive readiness skills, emotional and social intelligence competences crucial in leading organizations during the 4.0 industrial revolution (Bawany, 2018c).

Practitioners and researchers of leadership view emotional and social intelligence as the overriding factor of a future's success (Goleman, 1997; Menkes, 2007). Goleman (1997) claimed that emotional intelligence is more important than any other element for future leaders. Goleman distinguished five components of emotional intelligence, including the following:

Self-awareness – the ability to recognize and understand one's moods, emotions, and impulses, as well as their impact on others. Key features: self-confidence, realistic self-esteem, self-deprecating sense of humor.

Self-control – the ability to control or change the direction of destructive impulses and moods, the tendency to refrain from giving opinions – think first, then evaluate and act. Characteristics: righteousness and nobility, freedom in a situation of ambiguity, openness to change.

Motivation – passion for work not only because of money or position, enthusiasm and persistence in pursuing goals. Characteristics: ambition, optimism, even in the face of failure, commitment to the company.

Empathy – the ability to understand the emotional nature of other people. The ability to treat people according to their emotional reactions. Characteristics: supported by knowledge readiness to develop and promote talents in the company, sensitivity to cultural differences, kindness toward customers, and recipients.

Social skills – proficiency in relationship management, ease of making contacts, the ability to find common ground and build good relationships. Characteristic features: effectiveness in managing change, a gift of persuasion, the ability to create and manage teams supported by knowledge.

However, personality type is not an indicator of emotional intelligence (Goleman, 1997). Charismatic leaders often do not have emotional intelligence (personality and style prevail in them). Hence, they often pose a severe threat to the organization's survival, as they try to play the role of infallible and decision-making at the expense of correct decisions. The ease of clear thinking and open mind, or intelligence, largely determines leadership success.

Cognitive readiness can be viewed as part of the advanced thinking skills that make leaders ready to confront whatever new and complex problems they might face (Bawany, 2019). Cognitive readiness is the mental preparation that leaders develop so that they, and their teams, are prepared to face the ongoing dynamic, ill-defined, and unpredictable challenges in the digital, highly disruptive, and VUCA-driven business environment. Cognitive readiness is also defined as the mental, emotional, and interpersonal preparedness for uncertainty and risk (Centre for Executive Education, 2020)

The Executive Development Associates has identified the following seven critical cognitive readiness skills collectively known as Paragon7, which develop, enhance, or sustain a leader's ability to navigate successfully current times. The skills are as follows (Bawany, 2019):

1 **Mental Cognition**: Recognize and regulate your thoughts and emotions
2 **Attentional Control**: Manage and focus your attention
3 **Sensemaking**: Connect the dots and see the bigger picture
4 **Intuition**: Check your gut, but do not let it rule your mind
5 **Problem-Solving**: Use analytical and creative methods to resolve a challenge
6 **Adaptability**: Be willing and able to change with shifting conditions
7 **Communication**: Inspire others to action; create fluid communication pathways

Overall, heightened cognitive readiness allows leaders to maintain a better sense of self-control in stressful situations. The leaders of Industry 4.0 must guide organizations through uncertainties of the future, cynic political climate, creating a universal view of technology integration with the economic, social, cultural, political, and ecological environment, making nonlinear decisions (Bawany, 2019).

Leadership 4.0 Insights

The rise of Industry 4.0 has prompted leadership researchers and practitioners dealing with human resource management in the organization to consider new models. In the face of new challenges posed by the continually developing economy and technologies and changes in the approach to life and the perception of reality by people, it is necessary to redefine the concept of leadership and define its essence in achieving success in contemporary organizations. Several leadership styles in the Industry 4.0 era, known as Leadership 4.0, have emerged from the research conducted. Below, three of them will be presented that are most often described and discussed in the literature on the subject devoted to Industry 4.0:

- Leadership 4.0 according to Deloitte
- Leadership Matrix by B. Oberer and A. Erkollar
- Stanton Chase Model of leadership

Leadership 4.0 According to Deloitte

The research conducted by Deloitte and Forbes Insights in 2019 (Deloitte, 2019) among 2,000 of the surveyed CEOs of the largest companies shows four types of leaders who are better than others at adapting to the new reality. They are Leaders of Social Impact Leaders, Data Leverage Advocates, Breakthrough Change Promoters, and Talent Ambassadors.

The following features characterize the identified types of leaders:

Social Impact Leaders – these are leaders who believe that pro-social activities are fundamental to the company. These people effectively create new sources of income through socially engaged and sustainable products or services. They believe that such initiatives usually help to increase profitability. Social Impact Leaders are confident in their abilities to deal with the human resource challenges of the Industry 4.0. They claim that their company structure is more relevant to the needs of digital transformation and are much more willing to train their employees.

Data Leverage Advocates – strategic barriers, such as silo structures within an organization, can complicate decision-making and slow down the pace of innovation. Data Leverage Advocates overcome such obstacles by consistently adopting a data-centric approach, enabling them to be more confident in their decision-making. Such leaders are characterized by greater self-confidence – 62% of people from this group strongly claim that they have the preparation to manage their company using the potential of Industry 4.0.

Breakthrough Change Promoters – understand that investing in innovation is essential for development. These managers invest in technology, trying to transform the market altogether. The breakthrough change promoters' brave decisions pay off – their investments have already achieved or exceeded the intended business results. They more often feel ready to take the lead in the Industry 4.0 era and have greater confidence that their organizations are adequately prepared to take advantage of its opportunities.

Talent Ambassadors – have a good understanding of what skills their organization needs and believe that the company's current employment structure is appropriate. Such managers make intensive efforts to prepare their company for digital transformation; they assume responsibility for training employees for the future. Talent Ambassadors are also more likely to invest in technology to leapfrog the competition.

4.0 Leadership Matrix by B. Oberer and A. Erkollar

Oberer and Erkollar (2018) developed a two-dimensional 4.0 leadership style matrix that constitutes a response to Industry 4.0 requirements and conditions in leadership. Oberer and Erkollar (2018) claimed that some essential elements – abilities – determine Industry 4.0, who they call the digital leaders. The parts are as follows:

- **organizational objectives** – the ability to move from fixed cycles for assessing employee performance, up to the ability to understand that situations determine the need for evaluating employees and teams equally, with the ability to implement feedback routines

- **people** – the ability to distribute tasks based on the situation and team competence, linking the skills of managers and employees to form a competence networking intelligence
- **change** – high-level willingness and the ability for change, encouraging high-level agility between the market, customer, partners, and employees, and deliberating promotion
- **output** – the ability to control processes, evaluate tasks and results together with teams; to use resources according to competence – cross-hierarchical and cross-functional – instead of managing orders, resource plans, and assessing results within the borders of a project, as traditional leaders do
- **mistakes and conflicts** – creating an open atmosphere with the learning effect in errors and a collaborative atmosphere for handling conflict situations
- **communication** – the ability to create a transparent framework for information distribution, counting on employees' and teams' collectible debt of self-responsibility, and proactive behavior
- **innovation** – knowing that innovation is learnable, being able to transform old structures using multidisciplinary teams, and creative processes, and flexible work environments

As a result of their research, Oberer and Erkollar developed a two-dimensional 4.0 leadership matrix where the x-axis stands for innovation and technology concern while the y-axis stands for people concern. This matrix should help to choose the most appropriate 4.0 leadership style, based on the degree of innovation and technology orientation and the people leading. The types of leadership identified here are as follows:

4.0 freshmen leader – with low concern for innovation and technology as well as the low concern for people – is concerned with an ability to focus on traditional manufacturing structures with the primary focus on the finalized product; it has no employee focus, customer needs of minor interest, same for emerging technologies.

4.0 social leader – with low concern for innovation and technology and high concern for people – a person who is generally seeking employee commitment to decisions and prefers an employee-focused leadership style. It refers to an ability to create a friendly atmosphere for employees without regard to innovation and technology. Supporting employees is essential.

4.0 technological leader – with a high focus on innovation and technology and low focus on people. It is related to an ability to determine how new technology can be used to deliver enhanced value.

4.0 digital leader – with high concern for innovation and technology and high concern for people. It focuses on understanding how technology impacts people, and the organizational model is aligned with human nature. These are equally essential elements of digital leadership.

According to Oberer and Erkollar (2018), The "4.0 Digital Leader" leadership style is the most productive 4.0 leadership style.

Stanton Chase Model of Leadership

Stanton Chase (2016) consulting company observing the landscape and new expectations of leaders in all industries in the era of Industry 4.0, identified four skill areas that top leaders need in the digital age. These are the following:

1 **Traditional leadership skills** – while recent publications' focus reveals the need for a "new" leadership style and approach, this does not mean that the previous leadership skills are no longer necessary. Quite the contrary: traditional leadership skills – such as the ability to effectively lead, manage, and inspire others – are now considered a bare minimum requirement.

2 **Ability to create a diverse environment** – it is critical to successful leadership in the digital age. Diversity does not merely mean filling the workspace with different skin colors; it means welcoming and embracing a wide array of opinions, perspectives, and backgrounds. Great leaders intentionally surround themselves with those who disagree and can offer new and varied insights. This approach to diversity enhances a leader's knowledge and understanding of the issues at stake.

3 **Agile leadership** – it includes the ability to manage a multi-generational workplace. The new generation of millennials tends to expect flexible working arrangements and a more cooperative and communicative structure. Successful leaders must recognize and adapt to the varying needs of the changing workforce. The Stanton Chase representatives highlight five facets of agility: innovating, performing, reflecting, risking, and defending, all of which play an essential role in the leader's success. According to Stanton Chase, agile leadership is critical for leading today's revolution.

4 **Ethical responsibility** – is an increasingly key factor in determining a leader's success. At Stanton Chase, they have seen ethical challenges permeate the search industry. Many companies focus on soft skills and experience that individuals bring to an organization. A detailed examination of ethics is not often seen as a fundamental feature of the hiring process. Nonetheless, as they have observed, leadership ethics considerations can make or break C-suite leaders' careers.

All models mentioned provide us with a new vision of leadership and leaders in Industry 4.0. Now we know that Industry 4.0 is happening now, therefore acquiring new skills seems essential to lead successful teams and organizations.

Leadership 4.0 in the SME Sector in Poland

Scientists from the Faculty of Organization and Management of the Silesian University of Technology, Poland, conducted comprehensive research on the readiness to implement the Industry 4.0 concept in Poland's SME sector. The study was carried out from December 2019 to March 2020, among a sample of 553 randomly selected enterprises from the SME sector, representing various industries according to section C of the Polish Classification of Activities – Manufacturing. The research covered areas important from the point of view of company management in the Industry 4.0 era. In total, nine areas were analyzed, including the following: clients, leadership and people, products, processes, technology, support and development of entrepreneurship, strategy and efficiency, innovation, and organizational culture.

The research used a questionnaire, where most of the questions were marked with a five-point Likert scale. Several open-ended questions were asked. The respondents were mostly companies' managers or owners. The research aimed to identify the state of readiness of enterprises from the SME sector to implement Industry 4.0 solutions in their everyday operation. Selected research results in leadership are presented in Table 6.2.

SME are entities that, due to their flexibility and the possibility of quick reaction to changes in the environment, can respond to the opportunities and threats appearing in the surrounding. The conducted research showed that most companies that participated in the survey see the need and, at the same time, implement specific activities in the field of leadership to address the reality of Industry 4.0. The industry reaction is indicated by the high number of positive responses to the development and implementation of digital and social competences by managers and leaders of these enterprises (issues 1–4). Enterprises are not afraid of employing qualified specialists and showing a willingness to train and improve qualifications (issues 8–11) and express readiness and openness to changes (issues 13–14). They consider investment risk (issue 12) to be the main barrier to implementing Industry 4.0 solutions. Financial problems may also cause the infrequent use of management support instruments, either in the area of decision-making processes or in areas directly related to manufacturing, production, and business organization (issues 5–7). They can also be sources of lack of participation in training both in technology-related and social areas (issues 17–18). Nevertheless, the willingness to share knowledge within the organization (issues 15–16) and the awareness of the need to continually adapt learning to the requirements of the developing environment (issues 19–20) indicate the

Table 6.2 Leadership in SME in Poland in the era of Industry 4.0 Research results (*n* = 553)

Leadership issue	No	Rather no	I don't know	Rather yes	Yes
1. A leader with technical competences like, e.g., the ability of programming, coding, digitizing processes etc. is valued In our company.	66	50	85	150	202
2. A leader with conceptual competences like, e.g., forecasting and programming strategic activities related to the company's development and its relations with the environment is valued in our company.	49	29	80	171	224
3. A leader with interpersonal skills, e.g., conflict resolution, cooperation with an intercultural team is highly valued in our company.	56	45	76	167	209
4. A leader with personal competences like, e.g., the ability to learn and self-improve, flexibility in accepting and influencing changes is valued in our company.	27	10	52	196	268
5. Leaders in our company use modern management instruments to support decision-making processes.	348	79	64	43	19
6. Leaders in our company use modern management instruments supporting the entire production and procurement process (e.g., MRP, ERP II, MES, SCM, etc.)	295	75	63	48	72
7. Leaders in our company do not use any modern management instruments at all.	183	61	83	71	155
8. In our company, the main barrier to implementing Industry 4.0 solutions (including robotics and production automation) is the need to employ specialists.	127	103	150	98	75
9. In our company, the main barrier to implementing Industry 4.0 solutions (including robotics and production automation) is the reluctance to change.	194	125	119	72	43
10. In our company, the main barrier to implementing Industry 4.0 solutions (including robotics and production automation) is the need to dismiss some employees.	246	152	98	34	23

(*continued*)

Table 6.2 Cont.

Leadership issue	No	Rather no	I don't know	Rather yes	Yes
11. In our company, the main barrier to implementing Industry 4.0 solutions (including robotics and production automation) is the need to improve the qualifications of current employees.	139	101	91	158	64
12. In our company, the main barrier to implementing Industry 4.0 solutions (including robotics and production automation) is the investment risk.	81	64	125	161	122
13. Our company is open to changes related to the implementation of technological innovations.	13	19	28	215	278
14. Our company is open to changes related to the implementation of organizational innovations.	31	50	74	196	202
15. Our employees are happy to share their ideas related to the improvement and optimization of technological processes related to the development of Industry 4.0.	84	57	142	150	120
16. Our employees are happy to share their ideas related to the improvement and optimization of organizational processes related to the development of Industry 4.0.	89	69	154	144	97
17. In our company, employees participate in training in the field of ICT (information and communication technologies).	225	99	48	106	75
18. In our company, employees participate in training in the field of social competences.	219	105	67	103	59
19. Adapting the company's operations to the requirements of Industry 4.0 needs adapting the knowledge and competences of the company's employees to these requirements.	34	30	59	237	193
20. The company can carry out information and training activities related to the requirements of "Industry 4.0" on its own.	77	133	112	160	71

Source: Author's own study based on research conducted within the Industry 4.0 project realized on the Faculty of Organization and Management at the Silesian University of Technology, Poland.

overall positive result and a high degree of readiness of enterprises from the SME sector to implement Industry 4.0 solutions in leadership.

Conclusions and Recommendations

The Industry 4.0, already a fact, is currently affecting significant changes in products, services, production technology, manufacturing processes, the organization of factories and teams, customers, and stakeholder relations. This revolution will also affect the emergence of new business models, and hence, will force the development of new competences for team leaders and company managers. Now more than ever before, organizations will need great leaders who can lead companies to success. It is to guide human teams through temporary change processes, lead people, and achieve organizational goals in constant change conditions. The world of technology is developing at a breakneck pace, and the manufactured products are characterized by an increasingly shorter life cycle. The Industry 4.0 is redefining our lives and working methods.

Research shows that companies will have to undertake brave technological investments that will become the engine of innovation and breakthrough transformations. Therefore, they will have to carry out several activities to remove obstacles inside the organization that hinder the implementation strategy of Industry 4.0 (Deloitte, 2019). Research also shows that executives are aware of the need for change and increasing requirements for skills needed to function in the Industry 4.0 era – evident changes are visible even in the two years 2017–2019. There is also an awareness of the need to change the model of leadership, which must take into account, on the one hand, the constant acquisition and use of technical competences. On the other hand, particular attention must be paid to a man as an individual, with his or her own system of values, talents, competences, personality, and degree of independence. The critical model features of Industry 4.0 leaders include (Deloitte, 2019): commitment and willingness to work for society and development, databased decision-making, a bold, long-term vision of technology use, activities in the field of employee development.

The great challenge of contemporary leaders is to shape the company's strategy in such a dynamically changing world and define a clear vision of leadership. As the research conducted so far shows, companies do not keep up with formulating strategies for implementing new technologies – representatives of management staff do not hide their concerns about the variety of available technological solutions and the limited possibilities of the company in terms of keeping up with changes. As companies face these new realities, leaders seek the right approach to four key areas critical to Industry 4.0: strategy, societal impact, talent, and technology (Renjen, 2020).

References

Armstrong, M. (1999), *Jak być lepszym menedżerem* [How to be a Better Manager], Dom Wydawniczy ABC, Warsaw.

Aronson, E., Wilson, T. D., & Akert, R. M. (1997), *Psychologia społeczna. Serce i umysł* [Social Psychology. Heart and mind], Wyd. Zysk i S-ka, Poznań.

ASTOR (2018), *How to Define the Industry 4.0*, www.astor.com.pl/industry4/?gclid=EAIaIQobChMI86G3hLy15wIVxKiaCh2DkA1AEAAYASAAEgKx-vD_BwE&gclid=EAIaIQobChMI86G3hLy15wIVxKiaCh2DkA1AEAAYASAAEgKx-vD_BwE

Bawany, S. (2018a), Leading in a disruptive VUCA world (ISBN: 9781947843172). *Leading in Industry 4.0, Business Expert Press*. Expert Insights, New York, www.cee-global.com/e-book/abstract/

Bawany, S. (2018b), Leading the digital transformation of organizations (ISBN: 9781948580212). *Leading in Industry 4.0, Business Expert Press*. Expert Insights, New York, www.cee-global.com/e-book/abstract/

Bawany, S. (2018c), What makes a great NextGen leader? (ISBN: 9781947843189). *Leading in Industry 4.0, Business Expert Press*. Expert Insights, New York, www.cee-global.com/e-book/abstract/

Bawany, S. (2019), *Transforming the Next Generation of Leaders*, Business Expert Press, New York, www.cee-global.com/leading-in-industry-4-0/

Blikle, A. J. (2014), *Doktryna jakości. Rzecz o skutecznym zarządzaniu* [The Doctrine of Quality. A Thing about Effective Management], Helion, Gliwice.

Burns, J. M. (1978), *Leadership*, Harper & Row, New York.

Centre for Executive Education (2018), *E-book on Leading in the Industry 4.0*, Available on-line 15.01.2020: www.cee-global.com/e-book/

Centre for Executive Education (2020), *Importance of Cognitive Readiness as a Leadership Competency*, www.cee-global.com/cognitive-readiness/

De Pree, M. (1999), *Przywództwo jest sztuką* [Leadership Is an Art], Business Press, Warsaw.

Deloitte (2019), *Cztery typy przywódców w dobie przemysłu 4.0* [Four Types of Leaders in the Era of Industry 4.0], www2.deloitte.com/pl/pl/pages/zarzadzania-procesami-i-strategiczne/articles/cztery-typy-przywodcow-w-dobie-przemyslu40.html

Drucker, P. F. (1976), *Skuteczne zarządzanie* [Effective Management], PWN, Warsaw.

Drucker, P. F. (2000), *Zarządzanie w XXI wieku* [Management in the 21st Century], MUZA S. A., Warsaw.

Goleman, G. (1997), *Inteligencja emocjonalna* [Emotional Intelligence], Media Rodzina, Poznań. ISBN 978-83-7278-217-5.

Goleman, D. (2000), Leadership that gets results. *Harvard Business Review, HBR OnPoint*, Available on-line 20.03.2020: https://intranet.ecu.edu.au/_data/assets/pdf_file/0011/773867/HBR-Leadership-that-gets-results-by-D-Gole._.pdf

Griffin, R. W. Rusiński, M., and Mikołajczyk, Z. (2004), *Podstawy zarządzania organizacjami* [Fundamentals of Organizations Management], Wydawnictwo Naukowe, PWN, Warsaw.

Katz, D., & Kahn, R. L. (1979), *Społeczna psychologia organizacji* [Social Psychology of Organization], PWN, Warsaw.

Kouzes, J. M., & Posner, B. Z. (2003), *The Leadership Challenge*, Jossey-Bass, New York.

Kuc, B. R. (2004), *Od zarządzania do przywództwa. Dylematy władzy organizacyjnej* [From Management to Leadership. Organizational Power Dilemmas], Wydawnictwo Menedżerskie PTM, Warsaw.

March, J. G., & Simon, H. A. (1958), *Organizations*, Wiley, New York.

Maxwell, J. C. (2001), *Prawa przywództwa* [Laws of Leadership], Wydawnictwo Studio EMKA, Warsaw.

Menkes, J. (2007), *Inteligencja przywódcza. Co wyróżnia wielkich liderów* [Leadership Intelligence. What Distinguishes Great Leaders], Wydawnictwo Studio EMKA, Warsaw.

Oberer, B., & Erkollar, A. (2018), Leadership 4.0: Digital leaders in the age of Industry 4.0. *International Journal of Organizational Leadership*, Available on-line 01.03.2020: https://ijol.cikd.ca/pdf_60332_a88c6cbb2e0af05dcbe51c f06845b231.html

Renjen, P. (2020), Industry 4.0: At the intersection of readiness and responsibility. *Deloitte Global's Annual Survey on Business's Preparedness for a Connected Era*, www2.deloitte.com/us/en/insights/deloitte-review/issue-22/industry-4-0-technology-manufacturing-revolution.html?id=us:2el:3pr:4diGLOB1948:5aw a:6di:012119:4ireadiness&pkid=1005744

Robbins, S. P. (1998), *Zachowania w organizacji* [Behaviours in Organization], PWE, Warsaw.

Rutka, R. (2001), Kierowanie [Management]. In A. Czermiński, M. Czerska, B. Nogalski, R. Rutka, & J. Apanowicz (Eds.), *Zarządzanie organizacjami*. Dom Organizatora TNOiK, Toruń, pp. 75–134.

Stachowicz-Stanusch, A., & Aleksander, A. (2018), *Competences for the Future, Organization and Management Scientific Papers*, Silesian University of Technology, 121, pp. 485–497.

Stanton Chase (2016), *Leadership in the Fourth Industrial Revolution*, Gert Herold, Global Practice Leader Industrial, Available on-line 10.03.2020: www.stantonchase.com//wp-content/uploads/2016/09/Leadership-in-Fourth-Industrial-Revolution-1.pdf

Stogdill, R. M. (1974), *Handbook of Leadership*, Free Press, New York.

Stoner, J. A. F., Freeman, B. E., & Gilbert, D. R. Jr. (1999), *Kierowanie* [Management], PWE, Warsaw.

Strategor (1999), *Zarządzanie firmą* [Business Management], PWE, Warsaw.

Tannenbaum, R., & Schmidt, W. H. (1958), How to choose a leadership pattern. *Harvard Business Review*, 36, pp. 95–101.

Terry, G. (1997), *The Principles of Management*. Richard Irwin Inc., Homewood III.

Williams, J. C., DuBrin, A. J., & Sisk, H. L. (1985), *Management and Organization*. Southwestern Publishing, Cincinnati, OH.

Zieleniewski, J. (1976), *Organizacja i zarządzanie* [Organization and Management], PWN, Warsaw.

7 Skill Gap between Academic Learning and Employability

Huda Masood

Introduction

Business schools have experienced exponential growth during the past few decades within universities across the globe. They are often referred to as "cash cows" (Davis, 2009) due to the high demand for business programs compared to other disciplines. Despite this growth, there is enhanced pressure on universities, and business schools, in particular, produce highly skilled and competent graduates capable of adapting to the ever-changing and complex needs of the modern job market. There is a growing gap between the training business school graduates receive and the skill set required to manage their careers successfully.

Gone are the days when graduates anticipated a life-long career in a traditional organizational setting upon graduation. Social media and the Internet have given rise to the formation of free market systems (e.g., the gig economy) characterized by increasing career interruptions, growing mobile and global workforce, and independent contractors inside and outside of organizational boundaries (Lent, 2018; Sullivan, 1999; Sullivan et al., 1998; Eby & DeMatteo, 2000). Accordingly, a pattern of employment opportunities extending beyond the confines of a single employment setting is explained in terms of boundaryless careers (DeFillippi & Arthur, 1994, p. 307; Inkson et al., 2012).

In essence, work today is no longer bounded to a place and time but can be done from anywhere and is increasingly becoming decoupled from a traditional and physical organizational structure (Inkson et al., 2012). Such modifications in the design and expectation of work require more than just the graduates' technical skills (Lent, 2018). Consequently, the focus is to balance the demand and the supply components of the job market (McQuaid & Lindsay 2005). There are serious concerns about a widening gap between the contemporary work environment's needs in a mobile and globalized economy and graduate students' skills and capabilities (King, 2003). The gap has created anxiety and unwarranted competition around the job market. Therefore, the decision-makers are urged to place employability at the core of higher education policy-making (Sharma, 2020). Inkson et al. (2012) identified the labor market structures, occupational nature, identification, and influences of educa-tion, automation, and macroeconomic forces to be a part of boundary-focused research. They reasoned that the seminal study by sociologists (e.g., Abbott, 1988; Carr-Saunders & Wilson, 1933) contending that several factors lead certain professions to close themselves to all except a few.

Bridgstock (2009) noted the proactive role graduates need to assume to effectively navigate the contemporary world-of-work challenges by self-managing their career-building process for optimal socioeconomic outcomes. Employability skills are directly related to acquiring and maintaining work opportunities (Harvey, 2001; McQuaid & Lindsay, 2005) and comprise generic and discipline-specific self-management and career-building skills. It is possible to assume that career management skills are essential to employability. They determine the extent to which generic and discipline-specific skills would be learned, manifested, and used (Bridgstock, 2009).

As the discourse on graduate employability expands its horizons within the knowledge-based economy, undergraduate experiences within the labor market particularly stood out (Nicholas, 2018). For example, the "psychological contracts" (Rousseau, 1990) that were responsible for a steady exchange of employee loyalty and work stability have been replaced by an increased focus on the notion of graduate employability (Benson, 2006; Clarke & Patrickson, 2008). As a result of this shift, graduates today are expected to build and maintain their employability in an ever-changing work environment.

Most scholarship on the strategic planning of business school programs informs the distribution strategies on knowledge assimilation (Friga et al., 2003), technology management or context-specific skills such as entrepreneurship (Clarysse et al., 2009), development of generic skills and competencies of the graduates (Andrews & Higson, 2008), and even self-management and career-building skills of the graduates (Bridgstock, 2009). However, there is a paucity of research on implementing an employability agenda within business schools that can integrate the dis-cipline competencies and career-branding skills while preparing them to independently navigate modern career models (e.g., boundaryless careers). Consequently, higher education institutions' role in preparing students to embrace boundaryless careers upon graduation and the optimal pedagogical practices to enhance graduates' employability within the boundaryless career context requires exploration.

Parrish (2016) contended the model of higher education should reflect the anticipated drivers of the future of work, e.g., automation, artificial intelligence, and technological intervention. However, the labor market landscape (i.e., gig economy) cannot be overlooked when considering higher education's role in optimizing graduate employability (Sharma, 2020). The direct relationship between management education and the evolving world of business (e.g., globalization and the resulting internationalization, prevalence of technological intervention, rapid advancements of automation and artificial intelligence, changing norms of workplace, etc.) calls for a strategic overhaul of business education more than any other division of academia (Friga et al., 2003). Given the noticeable shift in the emergent labor market and job altering technologies, fresh graduates need to be equipped with "cognitive, creative, and social skills" for a better transition to (future of) work (Sharma, 2020, p. 2).

I will explain how business schools can best equip students to steer through boundaryless careers effectively. This chapter explains employability and boundaryless careers within the volatile and changing labor market that graduates encounter. It then explores management education in terms of its current offerings and introduces the idea of restructuring business school programs as (i) an initiative to keep pace with labor market changes, (ii) to equip graduates with employability and career management skills.

The discussion focuses specifically on the key determinants of happenstance learning theory (HLT; Krumboltz, 2009) to identify the core components needed to facilitate graduate employability in a pyramid schema. The chapter proposes several teaching approaches based on work-integrated learning (WIL), promoting graduates' employability within boundaryless careers. My goal is to draw attention to these approaches' theoretical and practical relevance in preparing graduates for a smooth transition into the labor market and managing career shifts within boundaryless careers.

Employability and Boundaryless Careers

As an interdisciplinary concept, employability is explained from different viewpoints (Sharma, 2020). A vast majority of scholars and researchers have discussed employability in terms of an individual's ability to attain and retain a work opportunity (Römgens, 2019). However, as noted earlier, the past few decades have seen a dramatic shift of career structure from stability and security to fluidity and mobility (Arthur, 2014; Lent, 2018; Means, 2019). Given the drastic changes in workforce trends, new graduate employability is often considered an indicator of their career advancement (Cabellero & Walker, 2010). "Policy shifts, socio-economic changes, and technological megatrends are orienting the modern societies to prepare for the future by using education as the key to pace up with the changes" (Sharma, 2020, p. 3).

Kirby's (2000, p. 37) report based on International Labor Organization findings discussed employability as something that "often requires competing effectively in the job market and being able to move between occupations as necessary. It requires 'learning to learn' for new job opportunities". Hillage and Pollard (1998) discussed employability in terms of individual capacity to obtain and maintain initial employment and gain new work if needed (Vanhercke et al., 2014). In essence, the seminal definition of employability emphasizes an individual's ability or capacity than the objective outcomes.

The boundaryless career model allows individuals to pursue employment opportunities beyond the constraints of any given occupational settings (Tams & Arthur, 2010). In such a model, the emphasis is on permeability rather than the dissolution of boundaries to encourage inter-boundary mobility marked by *boundary-crossing* rather than *boundaryless* career attitudes (Gunz et al., 2002). Gubler and colleagues (2014) presented a five-factor model for boundaryless career orientations such as organizational mobility, geographical mobility, occupational mobility, individual preferences to work beyond organizational boundaries, and rejection of employment opportunities based on personal inclination. Regardless of the nature of boundaries, i.e., physical (Sullivan & Arthur, 2006), organizational (Arthur et al., 2005), occupational (Eby et al., 2003), geographical (Inkson et al., 2012), or psychological (Sullivan & Arthur, 2006), mobility remains a pivotal component of boundaryless careers (Gubler et al., 2014). However, much research on boundaryless careers predominantly focuses on hierarchical organizations while ignoring horizontal or more networked organizations (Lingo & O'Mahony, 2010). Furthermore, there has been an over-emphasis on success as a developmental outgrowth of the boundaryless career journey (Ng et al., 2005).

Graduates' employability is also understood through several models, such as an interaction between the labor market and individual factors (McQuaid & Lindsay, 2005), work context within personal lives (Rychen & Salganik, 2005), and an individualized focus on a multitiered framework of self-perceived employability (Rothwell & Arnold, 2007). Van der Heijde and Van der Heijden (2006) conceptualized employability through a competency-based approach for recruitment and selection assessment to offer an objective overview of the construct in terms of field-specific knowledge and generic competencies. On the contrary, a subjective view of employability operationalizes it as a psychosocial construct with overarching dimensions such as human capital, career identity, personal adaptability, dispositional factors, i.e., proactivity, etc. (Fugate et al., 2004; Fugate & Kinicki, 2008). While both objective and subjective accounts are based on concrete empirical evidence, I focus on graduates' self-perceived employability to understand their self-evaluations of employment chances in the labor market, compared to the other approaches that may be well-suited in investigating for working individuals in employment transition (Rodrigues et al., 2018). Additionally, the given perspective on employability offers a broader and potentially integrated view on the other approaches (Vanhercke et al., 2014).

Empirical evidence supports the notion that perceived employability and self-career management can directly predict career mobility (De Vos et al., 2011). Rodrigues et al. (2018) noted that employability is a vital precondition for establishing new career orientations. I will also discuss higher education's role in advancing the employability and career preparedness of management graduates for mobility.

Business Schools Strategies for Boundaryless Careers

Employability agendas pertinent to postsecondary degrees remain a topic of debate in higher education and policymaking (Bridgstock, 2009; Harvey, 2001). A recent development on the revised role of higher education and employability agenda involves individuals taking responsibility for their career situations (Sin & Amaral, 2017). Mass higher education is "designated as simply meeting employers' needs for a trained workforce" (Boden & Nedeva, 2010, p. 50). Some have viewed employability primarily as an individualized responsibility (cf. Fugate et al., 2004; van der Heijde & van der Heijden, 2006). Such individualization of responsibility has implications for tertiary education institutions as they essentially shift into a "service provider for individuals, a resource for training, and indispensable for the improvement of employment prospects" (Sin & Amaral, 2017, p. 99). It is no surprise that tertiary institutions' primary expectation would be to equip students with employability skills under such conditions. Unfortunately, higher education can barely guarantee employment considering the past decade's dire economic circumstances and the shortage of employment opportunities (Sin & Amaral, 2017). However, meaningful reform to consider within the tertiary education landscape would involve preparing students to independently navigate the labor markets and equipping them to adopt boundaryless careers even at the undergraduate level.

Career management skills based on attributes such as adaptability and lifelong learning would play a significant role in designing university programs (Bridgstock, 2009). Nonetheless, empirical evidence suggests that student potential for developing self-career management skills remain unrealized in most publicly funded universities at large (Watts, 2006). It is suggested that most university graduates are somewhat under baked to meet the shifting demands of employment and training practices conducted by employers (Lamb & McKenzie, 2001), which may affect graduate career outcomes and future university attrition rates (McInnis et al., 2000). Bridgstock (2009) suggests an optimal preparation of fresh graduates for a smooth transition into the labor force and employability maintenance requires clarification of personal goals and abilities, understanding the labor market demands, and an ability to engage in the career-building process actively. Similarly, Jackson and Wilton (2017) noted that higher education institutions' missions have expanded from developing skills, knowledge, and abilities to fostering an enhanced sense of employability and assuring survival in a highly competitive job market for future graduates. The expanded programs, such as WIL, have become central to employability.

Work-integrated Learning

WIL is a pedagogical design to help students transition to the work environment postgraduation and even update their professional acumen (Kramer & Usher, 2011). WIL combines conventional or formal academic learning with practical exposure to their profession to effectively prepare undergraduates to navigate the labor market effectively. WIL programs employ a theory-to-practice approach to integrate disciplinary skills and knowledge and their applications in workplace settings through real-life problem-solving (Bowen, 2018). WIL is considered instrumental in developing graduate confidence in their employment-related capabilities (Billet, 2011) while maintaining an appreciation for the world-of-work (Wilton, 2012). Furthermore, researchers have noted a gamut of graduate employability skills enhanced by incorporating WIL practices (Coll et al., 2011). Such employability skills are now considered an essential component of undergraduate education as they stimulate graduate ability to effectively steer through the labor market (Jackson, 2016).

Jackson (2018) categorized WIL into two broad typologies:

1 **Immersed WIL:** Students are physically exposed to professional settings through business practicums, internships, and work placements.
2 **Non-immersed WIL:** Students in this setting are subjected to virtual placements, simulation exercises, and the industry or community-based projects conducted remotely or on-campus.

It is important to note that unlike alternative learning approaches, WIL is not a rigid strategy to turn students into industry professionals but rather a range of activities that tend to fluctuate and produce different outcomes depending on the discipline or context (Smith, 2012).

The literature on boundaryless careers relies heavily on self-career management. I offer a pyramid scheme based on the HLT to understand universities' role in preparing management graduates for boundaryless careers. In essence, the HLT proposes that individual behavior is a determinant of learning experiences in planned and unplanned situations (Krumboltz, 2009). HLT entails fostering adaptability within individuals with an underlying assumption that the workplace conditions are likely to modify (Krumboltz et al., 2013). Therefore, developing skills and career competencies are integral to preparing individuals for such a whimsical labor market.

Furthermore, HLT pays special attention to individuals' ability to engage in exploratory activities to extract favorable outcomes from uncertain conditions (Krumboltz, 2009). This component of HLT is further reinforced by cognitive career theory (Lent et al., 1994), which states that experiences that generate feelings of success among individuals may directly influence the breadth of exploratory activities an

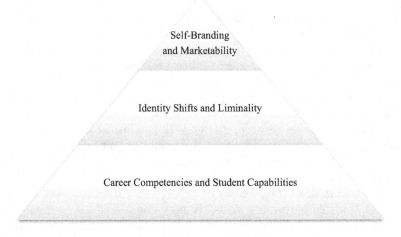

Figure 7.1 Nurturing employability for graduates through WIL: a pyramidal approach.

individual is likely to engage in (Krumboltz et al., 2013). This means that current management students are no longer expected to get overly attached with a particular professional identity but can experiment with multiple identity outcomes, which can be fostered among these individuals through strategic overhauling of business school pedagogical approaches. HLT encourages expanding the horizon of work identity; preparing for career uncertainty and change is critical in preparing for one's career path (Krumboltz et al., 2013). The final assumption of HLT is outcome-oriented and concerns individuals' actual achievement within the world-of-work (Krumboltz et al., 2013). Therefore, management graduates must understand the significance of professional branding in a competitive and volatile economy.

Building upon the HLT literature, I identify three core components career competencies and student capabilities (Bridgstock, 2009), identity shifts and liminality (Colakoglu, 2011; Nicholas, 2018; Jackson, 2018), and self-branding and marketability (Nicholas, 2018) to integrate discipline competencies and career branding skills in facilitating graduate employability in boundaryless careers (Figure 7.1).

I outline the components of graduate employability and career preparedness for boundaryless careers as follows:

Career Competencies and Student Capabilities

Hall (1996) predicted that employability would replace job security and that individuals would need to build new competencies pertinent to self-career management continuously. He described such a model as the 'protean career' and contended that such a career would dwell upon continuous learning. Hall (1996) further argued that such careers would comprise of a series of short learning stages focusing on individuals with know-how than learn-how skills. As the organizational provision of 'job security' has dwindled, individuals are expected to extract their work security through updated career management skills and their own and perceived employability (Berntson & Marklund, 2006).

Scholars emphasized the importance of acquiring new competencies that are essential to survive a boundaryless career. Such competencies fall under the three categories, namely: "know-why," "know-how," and "know-who" categories (Defillippi & Arthur, 1994; Arthur et al., 2005). Knowing-how competencies are the degree to which individuals establish and maintain a portfolio of transferrable job-relevant skills, knowledge, and abilities. As opposed to a traditional career that allows incumbents to accumulate employer-specific specialized knowledge and skills, a boundaryless career requires an accumulation of adaptable knowledge and skills transferred to other occupational settings (Defillippi & Arthur, 1994)—knowing why competencies refer to one's understanding of their career needs, abilities, interests, and inclinations. Boundaryless careers usually offer individuals more opportunities to become aware of their self-identity and self-concepts, as they are characterized by multiple mobility patterns (Colakoglu, 2011). Finally, knowing whom competencies entail developing and retaining a vast network of relationships that offer support, guidance, information, and influence to individuals—like the former two competencies, boundaryless careers entail increased opportunities to establish professional ties. Eby et al. (2003) suggested each one of these competencies predicted graduates' perceived career success and marketability. Another study conducted on MBA students corroborated the usefulness of knowing-why, knowing-whom, and knowing-what competencies within the context of a boundaryless career (Sturges et al., 2003).

As careers become increasingly boundaryless, management education can play a vital part in developing the central competencies needed to steer through a challenging and capricious terrain (Kelan & Jones, 2009). Although universities cannot secure or predict employment opportunities within the fields of student interest, they are still expected to directly contribute to graduates' employability to expand their chances of attaining meaningful work (Oliver, 2015a; Yorke & Knight, 2006). Most universities keep track of their graduates' promotional list of attributes, competencies, and capabilities (Oliver, 2015a). Recently, Jorre de St Jorre and Oliver (2018) demonstrated graduate employability in terms of 'capabilities' or a compilation of "knowledge, skills, personal qualities and understanding used appropriately and effectively … in response to new and changing circumstances" (Stephenson, 1998). Note the emphasis on self-career management in understanding these capabilities.

Nonetheless, it is not always clear how postsecondary institutions design their courses and learner experiences to guarantee their graduates can demonstrate the given 'capabilities' upon successful course completion (Coates, 2010). Therefore, there is a need to implement mechanisms to identify where graduate capabilities are assessed and evidenced in North American higher education model. I suggest higher education institutions can help students maintain a 'portfolio approach to learning,' allowing them to show their "learning derived from coursework including assessment artifacts—with other aspects of their lives, including work experience, volunteering, and so on" (Jorre de St Jorre & Oliver, 2018, p. 46). Gaining work experience during studies by taking part in WIL helps students fine-tune their disciplinary and nontechnical skills and enhances graduates' confidence in their capabilities while entering the workforce (Jackson & Wilton, 2017).

Identity Shifts and Liminality

An important dimension of employability deals with the extent to which individuals envision themselves in a given profession (Bennett, 2012). In essence, an employable individual demonstrates "a self that has been developed with the commitment to perform competently and legitimately in the context of the profession" (Tan et al., 2017, p. 1505).

Each job change within boundaryless careers entails a break or a liminal period during which relationships are severed and new ones created, old behavior patterns and responsibilities forgotten and replaced with new ones (Van Maanen, 1977). Czarniawska and Mazza (2003) argued that liminality had become boundaryless careers and individuals switching jobs continually. As with software that is not expected to attain a final version and, therefore, only beta versions are put to use and test, boundaryless careers are considered permanently beta (Neff & Stark, 2003).

More recent scholarship on careers supports the notion that employment no longer means maintaining a permanent job opportunity within a company (Rodrigues et al., 2018). Work is understood as a temporary state in long-term employability (Arthur & Rousseau, 1996) with individuals expected to manage their careers or develop marketable skills. On this note, Colakoglu (2011, p. 56) suggested that exploring boundaryless careers may enhance individuals' ability to develop a deeper understanding of their "self-identity and accumulate skills and knowledge that are transferable to other employment settings."

For graduates, this would mean not overly attach themselves to any given career identity as the chances of attaining all life-stages of a given career are limited despite their entrance in that career. This sense of future selves is viewed as *tentative trial-and-error thinking*, willing to transition through discursive and reflective experimental career possibilities (Ibarra, 1999; Nicholas, 2018). In congruence with HLT, which promotes self-directed exploration of plausible employment possibilities, management graduates are expected to craft trial selves as they navigate through a range of potential employment opportunities (Ibarra & Petriglieri, 2010).

Students view employability through the concept of optimal distinctiveness. They balance their undergraduate program affiliation and their emerging professional identities (Ibarra & Petriglieri, 2010). Higher education institutions can facilitate such distinctions by offering WIL cocurricular experiences or extra credentials to their undergraduate programs (Nicholas, 2018). Therefore, an implication here for business schools would be to provide opportunities for students to acquaint themselves with a professional ideology and continue to challenge them through evaluation and practice of knowledge and help them realize their beliefs and learning through reflection and feedback processes (Jackson, 2016).

Self-Branding and Marketability

Independent navigation through the current labor market insinuates graduates' need to manage their marketability and self-brand early on. Nicholas (2018) argued that marketable professional identity could change based on conditions among recent graduates. Such an individualistic display of brand development in boundaryless careers is crucial, especially for young professionals, to succeed within a changing landscape rather than relying on institutional promotions. While strategies and techniques of self-branding and managing self-marketability are considered at graduate levels (Kelan & Jones, 2009), it is important for management schools to promote students' brand value at undergraduate levels. Sullivan and Baruch (2009) contended that to be marketable, graduates need to adapt and repackage their expertise and skills to fit the labor market's changing demands. In a recent study on undergraduate students, Nicholas (2018) discussed the significance of projected employability on self-marketing strategies as students anticipate postgraduation work at the very start.

Therefore, the first step in self-branding suggests the question of self-differentiation from others, meaning that graduates must demonstrate the uniqueness and relevance of their skill set relative to labor market needs comparing to their other job-seeking counterparts (Holmberg & Strannegard, 2015). Self-branding is an absolute need for career planning and successful employment outcomes (McNally & Speak, 2002). While brands may not directly relate to the products or services per se, self-branding is essential (Featherstone, 1994).

Higher education institutions provide graduates with a social and psychological space driven by ranking lists and accreditation criteria to cocreate brands with students (Holmberg & Strannegard, 2015). Furthermore, contemporary management ideas of branding are often transcribed in students' self-concept and language pertinent to self-branding (Holmberg & Strannegard, 2015). The idea is that universities can essentially provide their students with a platform to visualize themselves as employable (Holmberg & Strannegard, 2015).

Teaching Approaches for Graduates' Employability

A significant challenge to facilitate employability is creating a culture that rewards academics' research activity in boundaryless careers through pedagogy (Lowden et al., 2011). Tyson (2005) highlighted that unlike students in conventional academic programs whose focus predominantly lies on acquiring knowledge, management students must assimilate their knowledge and skills to be applied in practical settings. Most professional jobs require an application of metacognition in multiple ways; henceforth, adopted teaching approaches should demonstrate such efforts accordingly (Yorke, 2010). Thus, to produce employable graduates, postsecondary institutions must rethink and reevaluate their teaching strategies within boundaryless careers. The following section explores teaching practices geared to address these concerns.

Constructivist Approaches

A common assumption in tertiary education scholarship is that a well-rounded undergraduate education with active student engagement levels beyond formal course framework imparts postcollege success for graduates (see Yorke, 2004; Pascarella & Terenzini, 2005). Traditional classes focus on case-based approaches, leaving skill development to others. In contrast, experiential learning approaches would integrate cocurricular modules and other special courses, emphasizing the impact of practice and feedback (Benjamin & O'Reilly, 2011). Although some may argue that employability prioritization and holistic learning under a neoliberal agenda of for-profit colleges and universities continue to remain compatible, it is, however, believed that holistic learning of certain disciplines (e.g., liberal arts) might directly clash with career-launching that matches graduates' technical skills with corporate needs (Roosevelt, 2006).

An indicator of such employable skills is the number of graduates entering occupations outside their academic subject area (Cox & King, 2006). Research has highlighted the positional shift between affluent students and their working-class counterparts when employability is enhanced through initiatives such as study-abroad programs, internships, summer jobs, volunteerism, etc. (Tomlinson, 2008). However, a significant issue with implementing constructivist approaches to gaining employability skills could be reflected in unpaid internships or other practices of labor exploitation. In fragmented economies where employment security is a major concern, graduates often find themselves in a position where they create work for themselves and others (Oliver, 2015b).

Maintaining a Multi-disciplinary Approach

Tushman and O'Reilly (2007) outlined that most academics end up confining themselves to their disciplinary expertise. Benjamin and O'Reilly (2011) rightfully probed an emerging issue of delivering effective education at tertiary levels through critically evaluating whether our academics understand what their learners need to know. Business school faculty are often faced with more challenges than other departments (Tushman & O'Reilly, 2007). The difference could be because business school faculty are expected to develop new knowledge with rigor and relevance (Tushman & O'Reilly, 2007). Also, given the competitiveness of the job market, it is simply not enough to equip students with hard skills (i.e., the knowledge, skills, abilities, and other attributes) needed for success, but also the soft skills (i.e., etiquette, professional deportment and mannerism, and elegance). These soft skills are critical not only for finding a job and navigating the career trajectory but also for effective customer service, especially since the service sector is the fastest-growing segment of the economy.

Minding the Pedagogical Misalignment

Program overhaul to meet the emerging challenges, especially if it involves revising pedagogical content at the curriculum level, may often result in a backlash as the retention of the traditional course content has been a common concern throughout higher education institutions. However, teaching approaches that carefully align traditional university values with advanced graduate employability skills can enhance graduate employability in the changing labor markets (Yorke, 2010). Therefore, one possible solution to pedagogical misalignment is to redesign courses, improving problem-solving skills through procedural and declarative knowledge building approaches that elevate students' ability to apply what they learn effectively (Benjamin & O'Reilly, 2011).

Fostering Learner Autonomy

Researchers have demystified the concept of learner autonomy through several themes: internal locus of control, i.e., learner sharing the responsibility or ownership of outcomes; efficacy beliefs, i.e., having confidence in one's skills and abilities; and self-regulation, i.e., implementing student-led learning (e.g., Macaskill & Denovan, 2013). Learner autonomy is also understood in terms of the surface vs. in-depth approach, where autonomous learners increase their knowledge base instead of learning through prescribed content (Thomas et al., 2015). All these themes are congruent with the commonly held expectations that postsecondary learners should distinguish themselves from secondary students through the active pursuit of an individualized educational agenda within higher education institutions (Thomas et al., 2015). In line with this view, Calkins et al. (2018) outlined how student autonomy may contribute to graduate employability through student agency. Ferguson and colleagues (2015) explained student agency as an individual tendency to take the initiative (i.e., through self-regulated learning). Similarly, students' perception of employability may be linked to their autonomy as learners (Henri et al., 2018). Taken together, we argue that developing learner autonomy through pedagogical processes will equip students with the confidence and independence to steer through the labor market successfully.

Conclusion

This chapter made a case for a much-needed overhaul in management education at tertiary levels. In particular, it argued that current approaches do not adequately prepare graduates to meet the challenges of an ever-changing labor market characterized by globalization, work mobility, internationalization, and technological intervention. The chapter argued that structural and programmatic changes are needed in pedagogical approaches to equip business school graduates with the skill set to successfully manage their careers. The chapter identified work-related learning models as a foundation for teaching approaches, promoting graduate employability within boundaryless careers. This chapter's purpose was to highlight the theoretical and practical relevance of the proposed guidelines in preparing graduates for a smooth transition into the labor market.

As I pointed out, over the past few decades, the debate on business schools' credibility and their teaching content has piqued (Khurana, 2007). Scholars have forewarned against traditional brick and mortar universities' downfall unless they adapt to the demands and rigors of a rapidly changing world (Friga et al., 2003). However, an increasing number of business schools continue to demonstrate meager shifts in keeping with specific technical skills and industry knowledge necessary for graduate success in the labor market (Clarysse et al., 2009).

As the labor market swerves from employment security toward the continuous task and role modification, new graduates are expected to demonstrate specific career management skills and proactively navigate the workforce changes to manage their career building processes (Bridgstock, 2009). The concept of graduate employability is built on the assumption that higher education is responsible for producing graduates to fit the labor market (Sin & Amaral, 2017). Employability agenda pertinent to postsecondary degrees remains a topic of debate in higher education and policymaking. An increased number of college students invest in tertiary education as a means of career fulfillment (Bridgstock, 2009; Karseth & Solbrekke, 2016). Education has long been conceptualized as a tool for effective navigation across economic and technological modifications (Means, 2019). Notably, a boundaryless career does not conform to traditional employment assumptions (Arthur & Rousseau, 1996). Therefore, the changes in labor market patterns in response to globalization, technological intervention, and competitive pressures suggest a dire need for adaptable workers capable of evolving their employment situation as the labor market and their dynamics change (Bridgstock, 2009).

Recent emphasis on employability in higher education has helped prepare college students with career management skills to facilitate their professional and social mobility and effectively cope with employment transitions (Bridgstock, 2009; Jackson & Wilton, 2017). It is essential to understand that developing employability is time-consuming and requires an accumulation of knowledge and skills from a diverse range of experiences (Jorre de St Jorre & Oliver, 2018). Therefore, mere completion of academic work cannot 'trigger' employability amongst graduates (Jorre de St Jorre & Oliver, 2018). Having a postsecondary degree in the current job market is no longer a differentiator but is considered a prerequisite (Brown et al., 2003; Tomlinson, 2008). Therefore, a core requirement in such an environment is to understand what, where, and how to demonstrate and transfer one's capabilities across jobs in a rapidly changing labor market (Jorre de St Jorre & Oliver, 2018). I hope that the ideas advanced in this chapter will open up a space for more academic debates amongst scholars, professors, and policymakers in higher education and provide a platform for future empirical research.

References

Abbott, A. (1988). *The system of professions: An essay on the division of expert labor*. Chicago, IL: University of Chicago Press.

Andrews, J., & Higson, H. (2008). Graduate employability, 'soft skills' versus 'hard' business knowledge: A European study. *Higher Education in Europe*, *33*, pp. 411–422.

Arthur, M. B. (2014). The boundaryless career at 20: Where do we stand, and where can we go? *Career Development International*, *19*, pp. 627–640.

Arthur, M. B., & Rousseau, D. M. (1996). Introduction: The boundaryless career as a new employment principle. In M. B. Arthur, & D. M. Rousseau (Eds.), *The boundaryless career: A new employment principle for a new organizational era* (pp. 3–20). New York: Oxford University Press.

Arthur, M. B., Khapova, S. N., & Wilderom, C. P. M. (2005). Career success in a boundaryless career world. *Journal of Organizational Behavior*, *26*, pp. 177–202.

Baruch, Y., & Bozionelos, N. (2011). Career issues. In S. Zedeck (Ed.), *APA handbook of industrial & organizational psychology* (Vol. 2, pp. 67–113). Washington, DC: American Psychological Association.

Benjamin, B., & O'Reilly, C. (2011). Becoming a leader: Early career challenges faced by MBA graduates. *Academy of Management Learning & Education*, *10*, pp. 452–472.

Bennett, D. (2012). A creative approach to exploring student identity. *IJCPS-International Journal of Creativity and Problem Solving*, *22*, pp. 27–41.

Benson, G. S. (2006). Employee development, commitment and intention to turn-over: A test of 'employability' policies in action. *Human Resource Management Journal*, 16, pp. 173–192.

Berntson, E., Sverke, M., & Marklund, S. (2006). Predicting perceived employ-ability: Human capital or labour market opportunities? *Economic and Industrial Democracy, 27,* pp. 223–244.

Billet, S. (2011). *Curriculum and pedagogical bases for effectively integrating practice-based experiences* – Final report. Strawberry Hills: ALTC.

Boden, R., & Nedeva, M. (2010). Employing discourse: Universities and graduate 'employability'. *Journal of Education Policy, 25*, pp. 37–54.

Bowen, T. (2018). Becoming professional: Examining how WIL students learn to construct and perform their professional identities. *Studies in Higher Education, 43*, pp. 1148–1159.

Bridgstock, R. (2009). The graduate attributes we've overlooked: Enhancing graduate employability through career management skills. *Higher Education Research & Development, 28*, pp. 31–44.

Brown, P., Hesketh, A., & Williams, S. (2003). Employability in a knowledge-driven economy. *Journal of Education and Work, 16*, pp. 107–126.

Cabellero, C. L., & Walker, A. (2010). Work readiness in graduate recruitment and selection: A review of current assessment methods. *Journal of Teaching and Learning for Graduate Employability, 1*, pp. 13–25.

Calkins, A., Conley, D., Heritage, M., Merino, N., Pecheone, R., Pittenger, L., ... & Wells, J. (2018). Five elements for assessment design and use to support student autonomy. Students at the center: Deeper learning research series. *Jobs for the Future*. Retrieved on April 25, 2021 from https://files.eric.ed.gov/fulltext/ED587401.pdf

Carr-Saunders, A. M., & Wilson, P. A. (1933). *The professions*. Oxford: Clarendon Press.

Clarke, M., & Patrickson, M. (2008). The new covenant of employability. *Employee Relations, 30*, pp. 121–141.

Clarysse, B., Mosey, S., & Lambrecht, I. (2009). New trends in technology man-agement education: A view from Europe. *Academy of Management Learning & Education, 8*, pp. 427–443.

Coates, H. (2010). Defining and monitoring academic standards in Australian higher education. *Higher Education Management and Policy, 22*, pp. 1–17.

Colakoglu, S. N. (2011). The impact of career boundarylessness on subjective career success: The role of career competencies, career autonomy, and career insecurity. *Journal of Vocational Behavior, 79*, pp. 47–59.

Coll, R. K., Eames, C. W., Paku, L. K., Lay, M. C., Hodges, D., Bhat, R., ... & Wiersma, C. (2011). An exploration of the pedagogies employed to integrate knowledge in work-integrated learning. *Journal of Cooperative Education & Internships, 43*, pp. 14–35.

Cox, S., & King, D. (2006). Skill sets: An approach to embed employability in course design. *Education and Training, 48*, pp. 262–274.

Czarniawska, B., & Mazza, C. (2003). Consulting as a liminal space. *Human Relations, 56*, pp. 267–290.

Davis, B. (2009). *Tools for teaching*, Second Edition. San Francisco: Jossey-Bass.

Defillippi, R.J. and Arthur, M.B. (1994)., The boundaryless career: A competency-based perspective. *Journal of Organizational Behavior, 15*, pp. 307–324.

De Vos, A., De Hauw, S., & Van der Heijden, B. (2011). Competency development and career success: The mediating role of employability. *Journal of Vocational Behavior, 79*, pp. 438–447.

Eby, L. T., & DeMatteo, J. S. (2000). When the type of move matters: examining employee outcomes under various relocation situations. *Journal of Organizational Behavior, 21*, pp. 677–687.

Eby, L. T., Butts, M., & Lockwood, A. (2003). Predictors of success in the era of the boundaryless career. *Journal of Organizational Behavior: The International Journal of Industrial, Occupational and Organizational Psychology and Behavior, 24*, pp. 689–708.

Featherstone, M. (1994). Kultur, kropp och konsumtion (Culture, body and consumption). Stockholm: Symposium.

Ferguson, R., Phillips, S., Rowley, J., & Friedlander, J. (2015). *The influence of teaching. Beyond standardized test scores: Engagement, mind sets, and agency. A study of 16000 sixth through ninth grade classrooms*. Cambridge, MA: Harvard University.

Friga, P. N., Bettis, R. A., & Sullivan, R. S. (2003). Changes in graduate management education and new business school strategies for the 21st century. *Academy of Management Learning & Education, 2*, pp. 233–249.

Fugate, M., & Kinicki, A. J. (2008). A dispositional approach to employability: Development of a measure and test of implications for employee reactions to organizational change. *Journal of Occupational and Organizational Psychology, 81*, pp. 503–527.

Fugate, M., Kinicki, A. J., & Ashforth, B. E. (2004). Employability: A psychosocial construct, its dimensions, and applications. *Journal of Vocational Behavior, 65*(1), pp. 14–38.

Gubler, M., Arnold, J., & Coombs, C. (2014). Organizational boundaries and beyond: A new look at the components of a boundaryless career orientation. *Career Development International, 19*, pp. 641–667.

Gunz, H. P., Evans, M. G., & Jalland, R. M. (2002). Chalk lines, open borders, glass walls, and frontiers: Careers and creativity. In M. Peiperl, M. Arthur, & N. Anand (Eds.), *Career frontiers: New conceptions of working lives* (pp. 58–76). New York, NY: Oxford University Press.

Hall, D.T. (1996). Protean careers of the twenty-first century. *The Academy of Management Executive, 10*, pp. 8–16.

Harvey, L. (2001). Defining and measuring employability. *Quality in Higher Education, 7*, pp. 97–109.

Henri, D. C., Morrell, L. J., & Scott, G. W. (2018). Student perceptions of their autonomy at university. *Higher Education, 75*, pp. 507–516.

Hillage, J., & Pollard, E. (1998). *Employability: Developing a framework for policy analysis* (Report No. 85). London: Department for Education and Employment.

Holmberg, I., & Strannegård, L. (2015). Students' self-branding in a Swedish business school. *International Studies of Management & Organization, 45*, pp. 180–192.

Ibarra, H. (1999). Provisional selves: Experimenting with image and identity in professional adaptation. *Administrative Science Quarterly, 44*, pp. 764–791.

Ibarra, H., & Petriglieri, J. L. (2010). Identity work and play. *Journal of Organizational Change Management, 23*, pp. 10–25.

Inkson, K., Gunz, H., Ganesh, S., & Roper, J. (2012). Boundaryless careers: Bringing back boundaries. *Organization studies, 33*, pp. 323–340.

Jackson, D. (2016). Re-conceptualising graduate employability: The construction of pre-professional identity in the higher education landscape of practice. *Higher Education Research and Development, 35*, pp. 925–939.

Jackson, D. (2018). Students' and their supervisors' evaluations on professional identity in work placements. *Vocations and Learning*, pp. 1–22.

Jackson, D., & Wilton, N. (2017). Perceived employability among undergraduates and the importance of career self-management, work experience and individual characteristics. *Higher Education Research and Development, 36*, pp. 747–762.

Jorre de St Jorre, T., & Oliver, B. (2018). Want students to engage? Contextualise graduate learning outcomes and assess for employability. *Higher Education Research & Development, 37*, pp. 44–57.

Karseth, B., & Solbrekke, T. D. (2016). Curriculum trends in European higher education: The pursuit of the Humboldtian University ideas. In S. Slaughter, & B. Taylor (Eds.), *Higher education, stratification, and workforce development: Competitive advantage in Europe*, Vol. 45. New York, NY: Springer.

Kelan, E., & Jones, R. D. (2009). Reinventing the MBA as a rite of passage for a boundaryless era. *Career Development International, 14*(6), pp. 547–569.

Khurana, R. (2007). *From higher aims to hired hands: The social transformation of American business schools and the unfulfilled promise of management as a profession.* Princeton, NJ: Princeton University Press.

King, Z. (2003). New or traditional careers? A study of UK graduates' preferences. *Human Resource Management, 13*, pp. 5–27.

Kirby (2000). Department of Education, Employment & Training. *Ministerial review of post-compulsory education and training pathways in Victoria: Final report.* Retrieved June 15, 2006, from www.det.vic.gov.au/det/postcomp/pdf/KirbyReport.pdf

Kramer, M., and A. Usher. (2011). *Work-integrated learning and career-ready students: Examining the evidence.* Toronto: Higher Education Strategy Associates.

Krumboltz, J. D. (2009). The happenstance learning theory. *Journal of Career Assessment, 17*, pp. 135–154.

Krumboltz, J. D., Foley, P. F., & Cotter, E. W. (2013). Applying the happenstance learning theory to involuntary career transitions. *The Career Development Quarterly, 61*, pp. 15–26.

Lamb, S., & McKenzie, P. (2001). *Patterns of success and failure in the transition from school to work in Australia.* Victoria Australia: Australian Council for Educational Research.

Lent, R. W. (2018). Future of work in the digital world: Preparing for instability and opportunity. *The Career Development Quarterly, 66*, pp. 205–219.

Lent, R. W., Brown, S. D., & Hackett, G. (1994). Toward a unifying social cognitive theory of career and academic interest, choice, and performance. *Journal of Vocational Behavior, 45*, pp. 79–122

Lingo, E. L., & O'Mahony, S. (2010). Nexus work: Brokerage on creative projects. *Administrative Science Quarterly, 55*, pp. 47–81.

Lowden, K., Hall, S., Elliot, D., & Lewin, J. (2011). *Employers' perceptions of the employability of new graduates.* London: Edge Foundation.

Macaskill, A., & Denovan, A. (2013). Developing autonomous learning in first year university students using perspectives from positive psychology. *Studies in Higher Education, 38*(1), pp. 124–142.

McInnis, C., Hartley, R., Polesel, J., & Teese, R. (2000). Non-completion in vocational education and training and higher education. *REB Report, 4.* www. researchgate.net/profile/John-Polesel/publication/237438336. Last visited April 25, 2021.

McNally, D., and K. Speak. (2002). *Be your own brand: A breakthrough formula for standing out from the crowd.* New York: Berrett-Koehler.

McQuaid, R. W., & Lindsay, C. (2005). The concept of employability. *Urban Studies, 42,* pp. 197–219.

Means, A. J. (2019). Hypermodernity, automated uncertainty, and education policy trajectories. *Critical Studies in Education,* pp. 1–16. Doi: 10.1080/ 17508487.2019.1632912 [online].

Neff, G., & Stark, D. (2003), Permantly beta: responsive organization in the internet era. In Howard, P. E. N., & Jones, S. S. (Eds.), *The internet and the American life,* pp. 173–188. London: Sage.

Ng, T. W. H., Eby, L. T., Sorensen, K. L., & Feldman, D. C. (2005). Predictors of objective and subjective career success: A meta- analysis. *Personnel Psychology, 58,* pp. 367–408.

Nicholas, J. M. (2018). Marketable selves: Making sense of employability as a liberal arts undergraduate. *Journal of Vocational Behavior, 109,* pp. 1–13.

Oliver, B. (2015a). *Assuring graduate capabilities: Evidencing levels of achievement for graduate employability.* Sydney: Office for Learning and Teaching.

Oliver, B. (2015b). Redefining graduate employability and work-integrated learning: Proposals for effective higher education in disrupted economies. *Journal of Teaching and Learning for Graduate Employability, 6,* p. 56.

Pascarella, E. T., & Terenzini, P. T. (2005). *How college affects students: A third decade of research.* Vol. 2. Indianapolis, IN: Jossey-Bass.

Parrish, D. R. (2016). Principles and a model for advancing future-oriented and student-focused teaching and learning. *Procedia-Social and Behavioral Sciences, 228,* pp. 311–315.

Rodrigues, R., Butler, C. L., & Guest, D. (2018). Antecedents of protean and boundaryless career orientations: The role of core self-evaluations, perceived employability and social capital. *Journal of Vocational Behavior, 110,* pp. 1–11.

Römgens, I., Scoupe, R., & Beausaert, S. (2019). Unraveling the concept of employability, bringing together research on employability in higher education and the workplace. *Studies in Higher Education, 45*(12), pp. 1–16.

Roosevelt, G. (2006). The triumph of the market and the decline of liberal education: Implications for civic life. *Teachers College Record, 108,* pp. 1404–1423.

Rothwell, A., & Arnold, J. (2007). Self-perceived employability: Development and validation of a scale. *Personnel Review, 36,* pp. 23–41.

Rousseau, D. M. (1990). New hire perceptions of their own and their employer's obligations: A study of psychological contracts. *Journal of Organizational Behavior, 11*(5), pp. 389–400.

Rychen, D. S., & Salganik, L. H. (2005). *The definition and selection of key competencies: Executive summary.* Retrieved July 1, 2006, from www.oecd.org/ dataoecd/47/61/35070367.pdf

Sharma, H. (2020). The nexus between future of work and future of higher education: Redefining employability and equity. *Medienimpulse*, *58*, pp. 1–21.

Sin, C., & Amaral, A. (2017). Academics' and employers' perceptions about responsibilities for employability and their initiatives towards its development. *Higher Education*, *73*, pp. 97–111.

Smith, C. (2012). Evaluating the quality of work-integrated learning curricula: A comprehensive framework. *Higher Education Research & Development*, *31*, pp. 247–262.

Stephenson, J. (1998). The concept of capability and its importance in higher education. In J. Stephenson & M. Yorke (Eds.), *Capability and quality in higher education* (pp. 1–13). London: Kogan Page.

Sturges, J., Simpson, R., & Altman, Y. (2003). Capitalising on learning: An exploration of the MBA as a vehicle for developing career competencies. *International Journal of Training and Development*, *7*, pp. 53–66.

Sullivan, S. E. (1999). The changing nature of careers: a review and research agenda. *Journal of Management*, *25*, pp. 457–484.

Sullivan, S. E., & Arthur, M. B. (2006). The evolution of the boundaryless career concept: Examining physical and psychological mobility. *Journal of Vocational Behavior*, *69*, pp. 19–29.

Sullivan, S. E., & Baruch, Y. (2009). Advances in career theory and research: A critical review and agenda for future exploration. *Journal of Management*, *35*, pp. 1542–1571.

Sullivan, S. E., Carden, W. A., & Martin, D. F. (1998). Careers in the next millennium: Directions for future research. *Human Resource Management Review*, *8*, pp. 165–185.

Tams, S., & Arthur, M. B. (2010). New directions for boundary-less careers: Agency and interdependence in a changing world. *Journal of Organizational Behavior*, *31*, pp. 629–646.

Tan, C., Van der Molen, H., & Schmidt, H. (2017). A measure of professional identity development for professional education. *Studies in Higher Education*, *42*, pp. 1504–1519.

Thomas, L., Hockings, C., Ottaway, J., & Jones, R. (2015). *Independent learning: students' perspectives and experiences*. Higher Education Academy. Retrieved last on April 25, 2021. www.heacademy.ac.uk/system/files/hea-research-seminar-independent-learning-slides_0.pdf

Tomlinson, M. (2008). The degree is not enough: Students' perceptions of the role of higher education credentials for graduate work and employability. *British Journal of Sociology of Education*, *29*, pp. 49–61.

Tushman, M. L., & O'Reilly, C. A. (2007). Research and relevance: Implications of Pasteur's quadrant for doctoral programs and faculty development. *Academy of Management Journal*, *50*, pp. 769–774.

Tyson, L. D. (2005). On managers, not MBAs. *Academy of Management Learning and Education*, *4*, pp. 235–236.

Van der Heijde, C. M., & Van der Heijden, B. I. (2006). A competence-based and multidimensional operationalization and measurement of employability. *Human Resource Management*, *45*, pp. 449–476.

Van Maanen, J. (1977), Experiencing organizations: notes on the meaning of careers and socialization. In Van Maanen, J. (Ed.), *Organizational careers: Some new perspectives* (pp. 15–45). New York, NY: Wiley.

Vanhercke, D., De Cuyper, N., Peeters, E., & De Witte, H. (2014). Defining perceived employability: A psychological approach. *Personnel Review*, 43(4), pp. 592–605.

Watts, A. (2006). *Career development learning and employability.* York: ESECT and HEA.

Wilton, N. (2012). The impact of work placements on skill development and career outcomes for business and management graduates. *Studies in Higher Education*, 37, pp. 603–620.

Yorke, M. (2004). Employability in the undergraduate curriculum: Some student perspectives. *European Journal of Education*, 39, pp. 409–427.

Yorke, M. (2010). Employability: Aligning the message, the medium and academic values. *Journal of Teaching and Learning for Graduate Employability*, 1, pp. 2–12.

Yorke, M., & Knight, P. T. (2006). *Embedding employability into the curriculum.* Heslington, York: The Higher Education Academy.

Part III

Educational Disparities

Regional Empirical Evidence

8 Automation

Differences in African Foreign-based Higher Education in Ghana

Obi Berko Obeng Damoah and
Anita Asiwome Adzo Baku

Introduction

As a result of the disruptive technologies (e.g., artificial intelligence [AI], machine learning [ML], big data analytics [BDA]) revolutionizing industry today (industry 4.0), higher education across the world is under intense pressure to incorporate ML and automation into its curricular, research, and other activities to prepare its students to fit the industry 4.0. Yet, in this ML drive, higher education in developed economies is advantageous compared to their counterparts in developing countries due to the digital divide. The chapter hypothesizes that the digital capacity of African-based foreign universities (ABFUs) will be higher than wholly owned African universities (WOAUs) because of the digital edge of the parent universities of ABFUs resulting from globalization higher education in developing countries. The study, therefore, compares the perspectives of Ghanaian and ABFUs in Ghana regarding ML. The results showed that the availability of capacity to embrace ML, the WOGUs far outweigh the ABFUs. Zoom represented the currently widely used ML platform by both groups.

Awareness of Automation in Industry and Higher Education

Following the advent of technological disruption in the global market place, the world of work is changing rapidly, including the skills required to do work. Changes in tasks, skills, career paths, and professions are among the workplace's automation results. For example, Kiselev et al. (2020) have argued that in today's 21st century, all institution whether or not it is a corporate body, nongovernmental and governmental bodies. The immense quantum of data, information, and figures for strategic decision-making transcends beyond human cognitive abilities and capabilities. Consequently, institutions embrace digital technologies' positive effects and make automation an integral part of their everyday operations. Digital technologies are capable of conducting independent search for information, patterns of communication and organizational interactions

(Chassignol et al., 2018). Kiselev et al. (2020) contended that browsing the internet could not have been possible without search engines, signifying ML.

Among the elements of automation influencing changes in the industry are AI, BDA, and ML. This automation is commonly referred to as digital technologies or disruptive technologies. Enhancing turnaround time, speed in responding to changes in the global market place, efficient input–output management, improved return on investment, reduction of production errors, and better management systems are among the benefits which accrue following using automation (Acemoglu & Restrepo, 2017; Fort et al., 2018). In labor-intensive manufacturing industries characterized by high labor costs, industrial robots have been used as alternatives for the workforce (Acemoglu & Restrepo, 2017; Fort et al., 2018). AI presents excellent potential in the industry because it could substitute and complement human intelligence.

People losing jobs due to automation in the workplace is becoming a concern for researchers, practitioners, policymakers, and educators (Ramaswamy et al., 2000; Shi et al., 2018; Frank et al., 2019). Researchers (e.g., Frey and Osborne, 2017; Sherman, 2015) argued that financial services (e.g., accountants and auditors), as well as jobs such as social workers, therapists, athletes, law firms, online marketers, diagnosticians, are among the jobs likely to be lost to automation. Kiselev et al. (2020) argued that counseling and guidance services can now be done incorporating automation, including consulting service (Kiselev et al., 2020). Williams (2019) concurs how AI shapes human activities by taking over jobs, thereby rendering most human experts unemployed. Researchers argue a massive demand for data analytic experts and data scientists to incorporate big data analytical software as critical parts of management (Shi et al., 2018; Lawlor, 2019).

As automation begins to create job loss to workers and future workforce, researchers, practitioners, and policymakers are becoming equally concern about the responsibility of higher education regarding the state of their curricula and pedagogy. The main argument is that if automation (e.g., AI, BDA, ML) dictates the skills required for the future of jobs, it remains imperative for higher education to respond appropriately. The reason is that increased education remains a crucial factor regarding the supply of skills to the industry. Consequently, there are calls for developing knowledge, skills, and competencies of lectures and students regarding digitization. For example, there has been an admonition concerning the use of learning analytics (LA) to enhance educational activities (e.g., global learning, curricula reviewing, individual and supported groups use of ICT for learning and teaching) (Herodotou et al. 2019). Therefore, digital technologies are embraced as a significant component in reforming teaching and learning (Huda et al., 2016). For example, big data in innovative teaching is becoming an excellent new experience for students, education providers, and instructors. LA offers the opportunity of implementing real-time assessment and feedback in education (Macfadyen et al., 2014). The student learning assessment tool is another application of AI in teaching and learning, where specific understanding in subjects is developed using concept maps (Jain et al., 2014). An AI-based student learning evaluation tool is used to improve students' AI techniques by evaluating how students understand specific subject matters (Jain et al., 2013). Ozbey et al. (2016) proposed a framework based on AI to analyze factors that affect students' learning.

Automation in Higher Education Curricular

One argument concerning automation and higher education is that higher education in the western countries (e.g., USA) are ahead relative to their counterparts in the developing countries because of the digital divide. According to Williams (2019), corporate bodies, such as Blockchain technology, train undergraduate students using an automated work system. William (2019) argued that participating in the training session aims to improve students' employability skills. For instance, most of the initial research and developmental works regarding digital computer systems begin at the University of Massachusetts Institute of Technology, the University of Pennsylvania, Stanford University, and the University of Illinois. As a result, samples of digital technologies can be found in classrooms and laboratories, including universities' administration in Western economies. BDA is also gaining popularity within the academic community worldwide (Laux et al., 2017). Various university records and instructional applications are undertaken using BDAs big data concepts and analytics. In 2011, the Austin Peay State University in Clarksville developed an automated system to educate students on their overall academic performance. Also, Georgia State University employed predictive analytics to inspire its graduation. According to Kurfess (2018), similar programs can be found at Baltimore's Johns Hopkins University and other colleges in the University System of Maryland (Kurfess, 2018). For instance, Northern Arizona University has implemented an early cautionary alert and retention system called the Grade Performance System (GPS). Ball State University also implemented a visualizing collaborative knowledge work LA system to foster cooperative knowledge-building by maximizing modern theories and writing, human–computer interaction, and science learning (Picciano, 2012).

Lecturers and students at the University of South Pacific (USP) in Fiji employ class shares by creating a space on the USP network. On this system, university lectures upload files which deal with information concerning a particular course of study for students to gain access (Raturi et al., 2011). According to Laux et al. (2017), this software was initiated based on predictive analytics solutions to assist students' academic abilities (Laux et al., 2017).

Stanford University employs AI tutoring applications to support lecturers in the tutorial room and students at their homes. For example, teaching robots were trained to remember students' code to enable deductive reasoning (Stachowicz-Stanusch & Amann, 2018). According to Stachowicz-Stanusch and Amann (2018), human–machine interaction can be combined with intelligent tutoring systems. The purpose is to provide a solution to scientific difficulties, facilitate learning a foreign language, and possibly support student-teachers in various academic disciplines (Stachowicz-Stanusch & Amann, 2018). Similarly, Harvard University has developed a chatbot that can assist the teaching of mathematics. In this system, the chatbot can resolve simple mathematical questions and offer information about students' progress and learning styles, including repeated faults (Stachowicz-Stanusch & Amann, 2018).

Other top universities in developed economies have also started testing some innovative approaches aimed at exposing students to upskilling strategies. Some of these innovative approaches are AI incubators, adaptive learning pedagogies, smart manufacturing talent education, and future project labs' factories. A list of some universities testing these approaches via automation is presented in Table 8.1.

As already indicated above, higher education is challenged regarding responding to automation, yet the situation is far less good concerning higher education's digital capacity in developing countries. Ejiaku (2014) noted that the implementation of technology in emerging economies

Table 8.1 Collaborative learning approaches – human–machine collaboration

Type of university and links	Project description/highlights
(1) University Carnegie Mellon University – USA	Runs variety of training programs in artificial intelligence (AI) in collaboration with the army in utilizing AI in health care, logistics, intelligence focusing on human–machine missions
(2) MIT – USA	Project description/highlights
	Explores human–machine interaction to engage students' interest in advancing AI and machine learning.
(3) University of Toronto – Canada	Project description/highlights
	Has launched certificate and degree programs training and preparing students in machine learning, data analytics, and AI skills. Also conducting research to provide practical solutions by applying AI.
(4) Colombia University-USA	Project description/highlights
	Offering degrees with a heavy emphasis on AI, machine learning, robotics, and computational learning

Source: Based on Ahmad (2019, p. 228).

is faced with numerous challenges in terms of funding, infrastructure, training, and culture. According to researchers (e.g., Au & Lam, 2015; Harris & Al-Bataineh, 2015), the few universities in developing countries that are embracing automation are just at their embryonic stage; yet researchers, practitioners, and policymakers maintain that higher education in developing countries has no choice to be left behind incorporating automation in their curricular. In the global economy, developing countries' students are competing for jobs with their counterparts from all across the world. Therefore, should higher education in developing countries lag behind automation, their students will not fit into the contemporary workplace and will be rendered jobless despite paying vast sums of money to acquire higher education?

With ubiquitous and continued globalization of higher education in developing countries, ABFUs are standard. Drawing on their digital superiority, ABFUs contended that WOAUs would lose their higher education market in Africa to ABFUs that are digitally rich following a spillover effect of their parent university abroad. Building on this line of argument and comparing ABFUs and WOGUs regarding their preparedness to align their curricular and pedagogy in the light of the digital revolution in the industry, particularly AI, BDA, and ML. Therefore, the extent of preparation of higher education in Ghana to equip students in automation to match the on-going digital revolution in the industry relative to the ABFU is the focus of this study. Consequently, the following research questions inform the study: to what extent do ABFUs differ from WOGUs regarding:

a   The degree of awareness of automation (e.g., AI, BDA, and ML)
b   The extent of usage of AI, BDA, and ML in research, teaching, and learning
c   The scope existing capacity to introduce AI, BDA, and ML in activities
d   Existing ML management systems being used

By addressing the research questions, we seek to make three key contributions. To the best of our knowledge, this chapter is the first Ghanaian study that compares the readiness of automation between ABFUs and WOGUs toward preparing the students to meet the digital challenge in the industry. The study sheds light on the topic from a new unexplored, unstudied geographical context, Ghana. Ghana has won a critical democratic credential within the West African subregion as the beacon of democracy in Africa and the gateway to Africa. Therefore, several countries within the West African subregion stand to draw inspiration from Ghana's shining examples. Lastly, this chapter contributes to the empirical literature field of higher education and automation research.

In the remainder of the chapter, we will (a) review the current literature on the topic and the conceptual framework for the study, (b) explain the method, analysis, and findings, (c) discuss the results, and (d) present the conclusions and implications.

Artificial Intelligence (AI)

One of the latest and fastest-growing technological phenomena that has enormous effects on organizations, including higher educational institutions, is AI. However, AI can be traced back to the 1950s (Popenici & Kerr 2017). Yet AI is gaining more attention in recent times; for instance, research on IA is growing on average at a rate of 12% per annum. The USA focused on the corporate sector, while Europe is more diverse. The share of the world's publications on AI from 2013 to 2017 are as follows: China 24%, Europe 30%, the USA 17%, rest of the world 29% (Lawlor, 2019). AI is a kind of algorithms or computerized system that is to imitate human intellectual processes, including the capability to generalize, reason, draw inferences, and learn from past experiences, just as do human beings (Castelvecchi, 2016). Ullman (2019) believes AI has a close similitude to actual decision-making prowess in human brains.

According to Hof (2013), AI has human-like features that make it process enormous, vast, and gigantic amounts of data, identifying patterns, speeches, categorizing images, and generating innovative decisions based on often real-time data. Popenici and Kerr (2017, p. 2) define AI "as computing systems that can engage in human-like processes such as learning, adapting, synthesizing, self-correction and the use of data for engaging complex processing tasks." AI is also defined by Iriondo (2018) "is the science and engineering of making computers behave in ways that, until recently, we thought required human intelligence." According to Chassignol et al. (2018), AI is the process of using computer systems to solve cognitive problems that human beings would have usually been doing. AI consists of computer systems that can make predictions and judgments that previously preserved humans' cognitive abilities (Williams, 2019). AI has become a cost-saving mechanism for organizations that can help these institutions employ fewer humans to do mental work using machines. AI can generate the most accurate information to make informed decisions, including producing similar solutions as human intelligence when it faces difficult problems. Whilst it was previously used in programming of games, AI is currently being applied in machine and robotic learning as well as professional systems (Ozbey et al., 2016). AI offers opportunities when used in education because of its human–machine interactions (Doctor & Iqbal, 2012; Ozbey et al., 2016). AI is applied in teaching and learning by way of fuzzy linguistic summarization technique which is be used to access performance of students.

Big Data Analytics (BDA)

BDA concerns the process of analyzing data to unveil patterns by deploying algorithms, programmers, and statistical modeling methods for finding relevance and timely correlations as well as associations (Chaurasia & Rosin, 2017). In other words, BDA is a large data set that is complex, multifaceted, intricate impractically managed with manual means, and traditional software tools (Baro et al., 2015). Big data has three key characteristics, namely: the size of data (volume), forms of data (variety), and the speed of data processing (velocity) (Sagiroglu & Sinanc, 2013). Here, the volume concerns the size of data; variety entails structural heterogeneity in the dataset, consisting of whether it is structured, semi-structured, or unstructured. Velocity implies the rate at which data are generated and analyzed in organizations (Yang & Bayapu, 2019).

BDA makes corporate firms become competitive and sustain the industry's dynamism (Goes, 2014). Big data's success is because it reinforces the organization's competencies by making them proactive in decision-making. In higher education, universities use big data for LA; thus, the coalition and data analysis to enhance learners and learning conditions. Big data provides lectures with educational content-related information, improving teaching, and assessment processes (Daniel, 2015).

Machine Learning (ML)

ML helps the corporate world adjust to the unprecedented rapid changes within the workplace and individual work career paths (Kiselev et al., 2020). By definition, ML is an algorithm to predict project performance (Sabahi & Parast, 2020). Mitchell (1997) defined ML as a computer program known to learn from experience based on a series of tasks and performance measures. ML enables computer programs to identify and acquire information from the empirical world to improve organizations' execution of tasks (Portugal et al., 2018). Although computer programs simulate human learning, the process of learning is not by reasoning but by algorithms. These algorithms can be categorized based on their approach to education: supervised, unsupervised, semi-supervised, and reinforcement learning (Portugal et al., 2018).

In higher education, ML is employed to enhance problem-solving. It uses language technologies and computational-statistical ML methods to robotically grade students' natural language replies. ML is classified as a subset of AI. ML refers to the process of granting a machine or model access to data and letting it learn for itself (Kučak et al., 2018). In higher education, ML-based assessment is used and it offers constant feedback to faculty, students, and administrators regarding how the students learn, including the support they need, the progress they make toward their learning goals. Speed in learning, accuracy, reliability, and simplicity are the benefits of ML in higher education.

Contextualizing Machine Learning

Palmer (2007) investigated the effectiveness of digital resources in the educational system. In the study, Palmer (2007) hypothesized that digital video resources improved management education and concluded that students rated the digital educational materials more highly. In another study, Lai (2011) explored how digital technologies in teaching and learning affect higher education in Australia. The result indicated that digital technologies respond positively to modification in the educational system. Selwyn (2011) explored the emerging use of integrated institutional technology systems in schools in England. They used qualitative-in-depth interviews on all schools' stakeholders, including senior managers, administrators, e-learning consultants, and internet and communications technology' (ICT) coordinators. In this study, Selwyn (2011) concluded that digital technologies were transforming the UK's educational system. In a study in Botswana, Mutula (2012) found that the automation project's impact increased access to the diversity of electronic resources, enhanced the image of librarians, and aided in freeing library physical space. According to Mutula (2012), library automation brought about access to electronic library resources from remote sites. Perrotta (2013) examined the perceptions of teacher benefits of information and communication technologies (ICTs). The survey included 683 teachers in 24 secondary schools across the UK. The result showed that teachers and students' most prevalent benefit related to digital technology are giving access to a broader range of learning content and resources.

Echenique et al. (2015), examining how digital technologies were used for social and academic purposes by students, found that students expressed high appreciation through the use of digital technologies because it enabled them to contact other students, communicate with each other over long distances, and share an educational interest. Dubey and Gunasekaran (2015) identified the desired skills for "Big Data and Business Analytics for education and training in a different study. In this study, the authors found that Big Data and Business Analytics have immense potential to increase organizational value." Maor (2015), also exploring the contribution of technology to higher research supervision in Australia, found that the digital pedagogy model brings about multidimensional changes. Using a social media application helps create the next generation of supervision pedagogy. Elhoseny et al. (2016) studied the automated information systems designed to assure quality in higher education. The result showed that the computerized information system collects and handles the data and information, which helps the institution's internal quality assurance system.

Besseah et al. (2017) surveyed the digital and research literacy support program for postgraduate schools in sub-Saharan African institutions. The study hypothesized that inadequate contents of information literacy courses are one reason why these courses are not embedded in the postgraduate curriculum of institutions in sub-Saharan Africa. The study's findings showed that information literacy programs at the postgraduate level in sub-Saharan Africa are not implemented, possibly because of the lack of content for these programs. Chaurasia and Rosin (2017) explored the applicability of big data in higher education institutions. They were using a qualitative research approach through a semi-structured interview. The authors identified four primary application areas for the use of big data in higher education. They found application areas consisting of reporting and compliance, analysis and visualization, security and risk mitigation, and predictive analytics. Furthermore, Makori (2017) conducted quantitative research investigating the factors affecting the promoting innovation and application of the internet of things in academic and research information organizations in Kenya.

Chassignol et al. (2018) researched AI trends in education. The authors found that the implementation of AI technology has offered many opportunities to develop massive open online courses. Assessment of many assignments, detection of learning, and teaching gaps have not been a problem anymore with intelligent systems. AI increases productivity in the delivery of educational responsibilities. Chaputula and Kanyundo (2019) studied the Koha-integrated library system by higher education institutions in Malawi. The study identified factors that negatively impacted the use of Koha in adopting institutions. These factors include lack of information and communication technology infrastructure, unreliable internet connectivity, and limited finances.

An exploratory study was conducted by Yang and Bayapu (2019), which investigated the data elements, transfer gaps, and the challenges of implementing data analytics in facilities management in the USA. The authors found that an accurate asset inventory can save time, cost, labor, and energy effective, and immediate access to information minimizes the time and work needed for retrieval and helps make an informed decision. The authors also found data analytics can broadly impact a decision-making process by transforming an intuitive decision-making approach to a data-driven approach. The data-driven decision-making approach can improve asset usage and lead to better predictive maintenance programs. Data-driven decision-making can also provide insight during budget calls, track trends for preventive maintenance, and provide supporting statistics.

Study Context

Ghana is a West African state that lies on Latitude 7.9465° N and Longitude 1.0232. The Atlantic Ocean borders ° W. Ghana in the south, Cote d'Ivoire West, Togo in the East, and Burkina Faso in the North. Ghana is known for its peace and relative political stability over the past three decades, and it continually ranks as one of the best democratic states in Africa. For instance, the Democracy index for 2020, published by the Economist Intelligence Unit, ranked Ghana as the sixth best democratic states in Africa. Ghana abounds in natural resources such as gold, manganese, diamond, cocoa, coffee, and other nontraditional export commodities such as mango, cashew, pineapple. Ghana is the second-largest

producer of cocoa in the world currently. Ghana has also begun the production of crude oil in commercial quantities.

Ghana Higher Education

There has been a significant and increasing demand for Ghana's education by international students, currently estimated to be around 10%
of total enrolments annually (Ayam, 2019). However, the mandate to
maintain academic quality in tertiary education in Ghana is vested in the
National Accreditation Board (NAB), a government agency responsible
for higher education management. As of June 2020, the NAB indicated
that there were 10 public universities, 7 Public Degree Awarding/
Professional Institutions, 5 Chartered Private Institutions, 81 Private
Tertiary Institutions offering Degree and HND Program 1 Distance
Learning Institution (NAB, 2020).

Research Design and Data Analysis

This qualitative research explored awareness of automation in higher
education, the extent of current usage of automation in teaching and
learning, the scope of the institution's capacity to embrace automation,
and the present ML management systems being used. We used the Likert
scale questionnaire items to solicit all the respondents (except the biological information) and aid our analysis. The respondents' background
information and that of the institutions were mostly categorical, as shown
in Tables 8.2 and 8.3.

Awareness of Digital Technologies

Table 8.4, using the arithmetic mean ranking based on the responses on
a five-point Likert scale, shows that the level of awareness regarding IA
and ML is much higher among WOGUs than their foreign counterparts
(ABFUs). Considering the awareness of two components of automation
(i.e., AI and ML) against one in the BDA, the case of the WOGUs, one
could conclude that WOGUs have more awareness of automation and
ML higher education compared to the ABFU. Overall, the mean for
both groups of institutions is approximately four, signifying moderate
awareness.

Automation in Research, Teaching, and Learning

Table 8.5 compares the perspectives of ABFUs and WOGUs regarding
the degree of their usage of automation in nine critical activities typical
of universities (e.g., teaching, faculty research, students' dissertation)
(column 1, Table 8.5).

Table 8.2 Demographic information of respondents

Variable	Frequency	Percentage	Cumulative frequency
Gender			
Female	1	5.88	5.88
Male	16	94.12	100.00
Total	17	100.00	
Number of years working in higher education			
6–10	4	23.53	23.53
11–25	11	64.71	88.24
36–50	2	11.76	100.00
Total	17	100.00	
Number of years in current position			
1–10	4	23.53	23.53
11–20	10	58.82	82.35
21–35	3	17.65	100.00
Total	17	100.00	
Age bracket of respondents			
31–35	2	11.76	11.76
36–40	3	17.65	29.41
41–45	6	35.29	64.71
46–50	2	11.78	76.47
51–55	1	5.88	82.35
56–60	2	11.76	94.12
61–65	1	5.88	100.00
Total	17	100.00	
Rank/position			
Academic officer	1	5.88	5.88
Associate professor	1	5.88	11.76
Dean	5	29.43	41.18
Deputy registrar, academic	1	5.88	47.06
Deputy head of institution	1	5.88	52.94
Executive director	1	5.88	58.82
Head of department	3	17.65	76.47
Principal	1	5.88	82.35
Program director	1	5.88	88.24
Senior assistant registrar	1	5.88	94.12
Vice president	1	5.88	100.00
Total	17	100.00	

Source: Constructed from the empirical literature by the authors.

Table 8.5 shows the use of automation (i.e., AI and BDA) in nine core activities of higher education. The WOGU employs automation in all the nine critical activities (i.e., teaching, faculty research, students' dissertation, students' learning, school-community relations, international faculty collaborations, international students' collaborations, creation of research centers, and students' internship project with corporate bodies).

Table 8.3 Background information of institutions

Variable	Frequency	Percentage	Cumulative frequency
Ownership type			
Private	13	76.48	76.47
Public	4	23.52	100.00
Total	17	100.00	
Origin of institution			
Foreign	4	23.53	23.53
Local	13	76.47	100.00
Total	17	100.00	
Age of institution since established in Ghana.			
5–10	6	35.29	35.29
11–25	7	41.18	76.47
26 and above	4	23.53	100.00
Total	17	100.00	
Focus of institution			
Management/business school	12	70.58	70.58
Wholly technology/management information systems/ICT/computer science	3	17.64	88.22
Wholly engineering	1	5.89	94.11
Other	1	5.89	100.00
Total	17	100.00	

Source: Constructed from the empirical literature by the authors.

Table 8.4 Awareness of automation in higher education

Digital technologies	Means		
	Foreign	Local	Overall
AI	3.75	4.15	4.06
Machine learning	3.25	3.85	3.71
Big data analytics	4.25	3.77	3.88

Source: Constructed from the empirical literature by the authors.

The mean for WOGUs across the nine activities was an average of three (occasionally/sometimes) as against two, rarely in ABFUs. The total average tilts around three, which implies both universities in Ghana occasionally employ automation in critical activities. Yet WOGUs outweigh the ABFUs. We realized from the telephone interviews that WOGUs are larger in terms of students' populations, with many staff doing different projects than the ABFUs.

Table 8.5 The extent of usage of automation in nine critical areas in higher education

Areas	Artificial intelligence (AI) Means			Big data analytics Means		
	Foreign	Local	Overall	Foreign	Local	Overall
Teaching	2	3.31	3	2.5	3.15	3
Faculty research	3	3.15	3.12	2.5	3	2.88
Students' dissertations	2	3.54	3.18	2.5	3.08	2.94
Students' learning	2	3.08	2.82	2.25	3.08	2.88
School community relations' projects	1.75	3.15	2.82	2.25	2.77	2.65
International faculty collaborations	2.25	3	2.82	2.25	2.69	2.59
International students' collaborations	2.25	2.67	2.56	2.25	2.62	2.53
Creation of research centres	2	2.62	2.47	2	2.54	2.41
Students' internship project with local corporate bodies	2.5	3.23	3.06	2	3.15	2.88

Source: Constructed from the empirical literature by the authors.

Table 8.6 The scope of the university's capacity to introduce automation

Current capacity	Artificial intelligence (AI) Means			Big data analytics Means		
	Foreign	Local	Overall	Foreign	Local	Overall
Department	1.75	3.15	2.82	2	2.85	2.65
Faculty	1.75	3.15	2.82	2	2.85	2.65
Current availability of allocated budget	1.75	2.46	2.29	1.75	2.62	2.41
Logistics/equipment	1.75	2.62	2.41	1.75	2.69	2.47

Source: Constructed from the empirical literature by the authors.

Scope of Existing Capacity to Introduce Automation

This section focuses on understanding existing capacity universities in Ghana, making it easy for a university to introduce automation. The result is presented in Table 8.6. The table shows the capacity of the WOGUs to embrace AI in terms of department, faculty, availability of budget, and logistics is higher compared to the ABFUs (i.e., an approximate mean of

Table 8.7 Machine learning management systems being used by universities in Ghana

No	E-learning management systems	Frequencies	Percentages	Cumulative percentages
1	Sakai	3	8.82	8.82
2	Google classroom	5	14.71	23.53
3	Voov	1	2.94	26.47
4	Zoom	9	26.47	52.94
5	Adobe Connect	1	2.94	55.88
6	Microsoft Teams	2	5.88	61.76
7	Skype	2	5.88	67.64
8	Moodle	4	11.76	79.4
9	SharePoint	1	2.95	82.34
10	Cisco Webex	1	2.95	85.28
11	Free Conference Call Mobile Application	3	8.82	94.1
12	Vcampus	1	2.94	97.04
13	ExamNet	1	2.94	100.00
	Total	34	100.00	

Source: Constructed from the empirical literature by the authors.

Note: Total frequency is more than the sample size (17) due to multiple responses.

three (somewhat available) compared to two (slightly available) in the case of the ABFUs. The same is true for the capacity for introducing BDA. Table 8.6 shows that the mean of 1.75 for each of the four areas examined implies that AI is slightly available in foreign institutions but somewhat available for local universities. Table 8.6 again showed that the capacity to embrace BDA in universities is higher (approximately three) compared to foreign universities (approximately two).

As shown in Table 8.7, the most common form of the learning platform by interviewed universities in Ghana is Zoom, followed by Google classroom, Sakai, and Free Conference Call Mobile Application, SharePoint, Cisco Webex, Adobe Connect are among the least ones. The variations between both groups are presented in Tables 8.8 and 8.9.

As indicated in Tables 8.8 and 8.9, Zoom represents the widely used learning management platforms employed by both groups. After Zoom, the learning platforms' order is Google classroom and Sakai exclusively for the WOGUs compared to the ABFUs that use Microsoft Teams and Skype tools.

Conclusions and Implications for Automation in HE

As we indicated in the introductory subsection of this chapter, the revolution of automation (e.g., AI, ML, BDA) and industry and its impact on higher education is widespread (Chassignol et al., 2018; Williams,

Table 8.8 Machine learning platforms used by ABFUs

No	E-learning management systems	Frequency	Percentages
1	Sakai	0	0.00
2	Google classroom	0	0.00
3	Voov	0	0.00
4	Zoom	3	75.00
5	Adobe Connect	1	25.00
6	Microsoft Teams	2	50.00
7	Skype	2	50.00
8	Moodle	2	50.00
9	SharePoint	1	25.00
10	Cisco Webex	0	0.00
11	Free Conference Call Mobile Application	0	0.00
12	Vcampus	0	0.00
13	ExamNet	0	0.00

Source: Constructed from the empirical literature by the authors.

Table 8.9 Machine learning platform used by WOGUs

No	E-learning management systems	Frequency	Percentages
1	Sakai	3	23.08
2	Google classroom	5	38.46
3	Voov	1	7.69
4	Zoom	6	46.15
5	Adobe Connect	0	0.00
6	Microsoft Teams	0	0.00
7	Skype	0	0.00
8	Moodle	2	15.38
9	SharePoint	0	0.00
10	Cisco Webex	1	7.69
11	Free Conference Call Mobile Application	3	23.08
12	Vcampus	1	7.69
13	ExamNet	1	7.69

Source: Constructed from the empirical literature by the authors.

2019; Kiselev et al., 2020). Also, job loss following the advent of automation in the industry is well documented (Williams 2019; Kiselev et al., 2020). Consequently, in most higher education institutions in the developed economies, LA is gaining momentum (Macfadyen et al., 2014; Jain et al., 2014; Laux et al., 2017) through the initiative of most universities. However, wholly owned local universities in Ghana possess higher awareness than foreign-based African universities (Table 8.3). In total, the understanding in both ABFUs and the WOGUs is moderate.

The awareness does not reflect the trend in the literature; a plausible explanation of the trend in Ghana could be that globalization of companies is few in Ghana compared to Western countries, so the automated industry revolution is also mild compared to Western countries. It would have expected that foreign-based African universities will be too familiar with automation and ML in higher education. Yet, the results show that even local universities are better. The difference can be explained by digitization momentum being relaxed in developing countries both in industry and universities. It is assumed ABFUs are caught up in the laxity and are therefore not an authentic replication of their parent university abroad.

This chapter explored the degree Ghanaian higher education uses automation in nine key activities (see Table 8.4). The results further yielded a shocking development that WOGUs were employing more automation and ML than ABFUs. However, the overall total average tilted around a mean of 3.0, which implies universities in Ghana occasionally use automation in critical activities.

The evidence in the literature shows universities have started initiating ML (e.g., AI, BDA) and others in their curricula (Laux et al., 2017). Some of the universities initiating ML include Austin Peay State University in Clarksville (the automated system that educates students on their overall academic performance), Georgia State University (predictive analytics that inspires its graduation), Northern Arizona University (early cautionary alert and retention system called the GPS), Ball State University (visualizing collaborative knowledge work LA aimed at fostering cooperative knowledge-building) (Picciano, 2012). According to Kurfess (2018), similar initiatives can be found at Baltimore's Johns Hopkins University and other colleges in the University System of Maryland (Kurfess, 2018). Other institutions that have followed suit include the USP in Fiji (employing class shares by creating a space on the USP network) (Raturi et al., 2011), Stanford University (using intelligent tutoring applications to support lecturers in the tutorial room and students) (Stachowicz-Stanusch & Amann, 2018), Harvard University (development chatbot that can assist the teaching of mathematics) (Stachowicz-Stanusch & Amann, 2018) (see also Table 8.1 for further initiatives by other universities in ML and automation).

Regarding which aspects of the nine activities universities in Ghana employ automation and ML, the telephone interviews showed that compared to faculty, students' local universities' population is larger than the foreign ones. One would have thought that at least using ML regarding faculty and students' international collaborations, the ABFUs will be ahead of the local universities because their parent universities would have made international exchange easy, yet the opposite became the case. Regarding the current preparedness to embrace ML in curricular, the WOGUs' capacity and preparedness far outweigh the ABFUs. In terms of the profile of ML currently being used in Ghana, Zoom represents the widely used ML management platform being used by both groups. However, Google classroom and Sakai were found to be used exclusively by the WOGUs, while Microsoft Teams and Skype were also found with ABFUs.

Higher education worldwide cannot be exempted from the influence of automation and ML because of its potential effect on the career prospects of their students who have to compete globally. Although the momentum seems to be high among universities in the developed world, the picture is low in developing countries (e.g., Ghana), even surprisingly low among ABFUs compared to the local universities. Throughout this chapter, we attempted to shed light on the awareness of ML and automation, including the extent of using ML in teaching, faculty research, students' dissertation, students' learning, school-community relations, international faculty collaborations, international students' collaborations, creation of research centers, and students' internship project with local corporate bodies. Our findings run counter to existing literature initiatives (e.g., Raturi et al., 2011; Kurfess, 2018; Laux et al., 2017; Stachowicz-Stanusch & Amann, 2018).

It appears investment automation and ML is a challenging task for universities in developing countries. Still, because this is becoming a key driver in the higher education industry globally, public policy must assist the local university in investing and building capacities in ML, massive data analytics, and AI. The results showed in terms of awareness, degree of usage, and preparedness in ML, the WOGU ranked higher compared to the foreign universities operating in Ghana. Meanwhile, the respondents of the study were top management of all the universities that responded. Therefore, we recommend University in Ghana, especially the Ghanaian-based foreign universities, taking immediate practical steps to build their ML profile, which will make their graduates more employable.

References

Acemoglu, D., & Restrepo, P. (2017). Robots and jobs: Evidence from the US. *NBER Working Paper No, 23285.*

Ahmad, T. (2019). Scenario-based approach to re-imagining the future of higher education which prepares students for the future of work. *Higher Education, Skills and Work-Based Learning, 1*(1), pp. 217–238.

Au, M., & Lam, J. (2015). Social media education: Barriers and critical issues. In Melani Au, Jeanne Lam, Radar Chan (Eds.) *Technology in Education. Transforming educational practices with technology,* pp. 199–205.

Ayam, J. R. A. (2019). The impact of Ghana's HE governance and regulatory framework on financial sustainability. *International Journal of African Higher Education, 6*(1), pp. 121–139.

Baro, E., Degoul, S., Beuscart, R., & Chazard, E. (2015). Toward a literature-driven definition of big data in healthcare. *BioMed Research International,* pp. 1–9.

Besseah, B., Achiro, D., Mhando, J., & Salau, S. A. (2017). Embedding digital and research-literacy support program into postgraduate studies curriculum postgraduate schools. *Library Review* 66(8), pp. 586–594. https://doi.org/10.1108/LR-02-2017-0012

Castelvecchi, D. (2016). Can we open the black box of AI? *Nature News*, 538(7623), pp. 20–23.

Chaputula, A., & Kanyundo, A. (2019). Use of Koha-integrated library system by higher education institutions in Malawi. *Digital Library Perspectives*, 35(3/4), pp. 117–141.

Chassignol, M., Khoroshavin, A., Klimova, A., & Bilyatdinova, A. (2018). Artificial intelligence trends in education: A narrative overview. *Procedia Computer Science, 136*, pp. 16–24.

Chaurasia, S. S., & Rosin, A. F. (2017). From big data to big impact: Analytics for teaching and learning in higher education. *Industrial and Commercial Training, 49*(7–8), pp. 321–328.

Daniel, B. (2015). Big data and analytics in higher education: Opportunities and challenges. *British Journal of Educational Technology, 46*(5), pp. 904–920.

Doctor, F., & Iqbal, R. (2012). An intelligent framework for monitoring student performance using fuzzy rule-based linguistic summarisation. In *2012 IEEE International Conference on Fuzzy Systems*, pp. 1–8. IEEE.

Dubey, R., & Gunasekaran, A. (2015). Education and training for successful career in big data and business analytics. *Industrial and Commercial Training, 47*(4), pp. 174–181.

Echenique, E. G., Molías, L. M., & Bullen, M. (2015). Students in higher education: Social and academic uses of digital technology. *International Journal of Educational Technology in Higher Education, 12*(1), pp. 25–37.

Ejiaku, S. A. (2014). Technology adoption: Issues and challenges in information technology adoption in emerging economies. *Journal of International Technology and Information Management, 23*(2), p. 5.

Elhoseny, M., Metawa, N., & Hassanien, A. E. (2016, December). An automated information system to ensure quality in higher education institutions. In *2016 12th International Computer Engineering Conference (ICENCO)*, pp. 196–201.

Fort, T. C., Pierce, J. R., & Schott, P. K. (2018). New perspectives on the decline of us manufacturing employment. *Journal of Economic Perspectives, 32*(2), pp. 47–72.

Frank, A. G., Dalenogare, L. S., & Ayala, N. F. (2019). Industry 4.0 technologies: Implementation patterns in manufacturing companies. *International Journal of Production Economics, 210*, pp. 15–26.

Frey, C. B., & Osborne, M. A. (2017). The future of employment: How susceptible are jobs to computerisation? *Technological Forecasting and Social Change, 114*, pp. 254–280.

Goes, P. B. (2014). Design science research in top information systems journals. *MIS Quarterly: Management Information Systems, 38*(1), pp. 3–8.

Harris, J., & Al-Bataineh, A. (2015). One to one technology and its effect on student academic achievement and motivation. In *Proceedings of Global Learn Berlin 2015: Global Conference on Learning and Technology* (pp. 579–584). Berlin, Germany: Association for the Advancement of Computing in Education (AACE). Retrieved April 28, 2021. from https://www.learntechlib.org/primary/p/150906/.

Herodotou, C., Rienties, B., Boroowa, A., Zdrahal, Z., & Hlosta, M. (2019). A large-scale implementation of predictive learning analytics in higher education:

the teachers' role and perspective. *Educational Technology Research and Development*, 67(5), pp. 1273–1306.

Hof, R. D. (2013). Deep Learning Retrieved from MIT Technology Review. www.technologyreview.com/s/513696/deep-learning/.

Huda, M., Anshari, M., Almunawar, M. N., Shahrill, M., Tan, A., Jaidin, J. H., … & Masri, M. (2016). Innovative teaching in higher education: The big data approach. *TOJET*, special issue, pp. 1210–1216, available at: www.researchgate.net/profile/Miftachul-Huda/publication/311576765_Innovative_Teaching_in_Higher_Education_The_Big_Data_Approach/links/584e7f5f08ae4bc8993779eb/Innovative-Teaching-in-Higher-Education-The-Big-Data-Approach.pdf

Iriondo, R. (2018). Machine learning vs. AI, important differences between them, *Data Driven Investor*, available at: https://medium.com/datadriveninvestor/differences-between-ai-and-machine-learning-and-why-it-matters-1255b182fc6, accessed October 12, 2019

Jain, G. P., Gurupur, V. P., & Faulkenberry, E. D. (2013, March). Artificial intelligence-based student learning evaluation tool. In *2013 IEEE Global Engineering Education Conference (EDUCON)*, pp. 751–756. IEEE.

Jain, G. P., Gurupur, V. P., Schroeder, J. L., & Faulkenberry, E. D. (2014). Artificial intelligence-based student learning evaluation: a concept map-based approach for analyzing a student's understanding of a topic. *IEEE Transactions on Learning Technologies*, 7(3), pp. 267–279.

Kiselev, P., Kiselev, B., Matsuta, V., Feshchenko, A., Bogdanovskaya, I., & Kosheleva, A. (2020). Career guidance based on machine learning: social networks in professional identity construction. *Procedia Computer Science*, 169, pp. 158–163.

Kučak, D., Juričić, V., & Đambić, G. (2018). Machine learning in education – A survey of current research trends. *Annals of DAAAM & Proceedings*, 29(1), pp. 0406–0410.

Kurfess, T. R. (Ed.). (2018). *Robotics and automation handbook*. Washington, DC: CRC Press.

Lai, K. W. (2011). Digital technology and the culture of teaching and learning in higher education. *Australasian Journal of Educational Technology*, 27(8), pp. 1263–1275.

Laux, C., Li, N., Seliger, C., & Springer, J. (2017). Impacting big data analytics in higher education through Six Sigma techniques. *International Journal of Productivity and Performance Management*, 66(5), pp. 662–679.

Lawlor, B. (2019). An overview of the NFAIS conference: Artificial intelligence: Finding its place in research, discovery, and scholarly publishing. *Information Services & Use*, 39(4), pp. 249–280.

Macfadyen, L. P., Dawson, S., Pardo, A., & Gaševic, D. (2014). Embracing big data in complex educational systems: The learning analytics imperative and the policy challenge. *Research & Practice in Assessment*, 9, pp. 17–28.

Makori, E. O. (2017). Promoting innovation and application of internet of things in academic and research information organizations. *Library Review*, 66(8–9), pp. 655–678.

Maor, D. (2015). The impact of digital technology on postgraduate supervision. In T. Reiners, B. R. von Konsky, D. Gibson, V. Chang, L. Irving, & K. Clarke (Eds.), *Globally Connected, Digitally Enabled. Proceedings ascilite 2015 in Perth*, pp. 688–691.

Mitchell, T. M. (1997). *Machine Learning.* New York: McGraw-Hill Higher Education.

Mutula, S. M. (2012). Library automation in sub-Saharan Africa: Case study of the University of Botswana. *Program, 46*(3), pp. 292–307. https://doi.org/10.1108/00330331211244832

National Accreditation Board (NAB) (2020, June 8). *Accredited Institutions.* Retrieved from http://nab.gov.gh/accredited_institution

Ozbey, N., Karakose, M., & Ucar, A. (2016, September). The determination and analysis of factors affecting student learning by artificial intelligence in higher education. In *2016 15th International Conference on Information Technology Based Higher Education and Training (ITHET)*, pp. 1–6.

Palmer, S. (2007). An evaluation of streaming digital video resources in on-and off-campus engineering management education. *Computers & Education, 49*(2), pp. 297–308.

Perrotta, C. (2013). Do school-level factors influence the educational benefits of digital technology? A critical analysis of teachers' perceptions. *British Journal of Educational Technology, 44*(2), pp. 314–327.

Picciano, A. G. (2012). The evolution of big data and learning analytics in American higher education. *Journal of Asynchronous Learning Networks, 16*(3), pp. 9–20.

Popenici, S. A., & Kerr, S. (2017). Exploring the impact of artificial intelligence on teaching and learning in higher education. *Research and Practice in Technology Enhanced Learning, 12*(1), p. 22.

Portugal, I., Alencar, P., & Cowan, D. (2018). The use of machine learning algorithms in recommender systems: A systematic review. *Expert Systems with Applications, 97*, pp. 205–227.

Ramaswamy, S., Rastogi, R., & Shim, K. (2000, May). Efficient algorithms for mining outliers from large data sets. In *Proceedings of the 2000 ACM SIGMOD International Conference on Management of Data*, pp. 427–438.

Raturi, S., Hogan, R., & Thaman, K. H. (2011). Learners' access to tools and experience with technology at the University of the South Pacific: Readiness for e-learning. *Australasian Journal of Educational Technology, 27*(3), pp. 411–427.

Sabahi, S., & Parast, M. M. (2020). The impact of entrepreneurship orientation on project performance: A machine learning approach. *International Journal of Production Economics, 226*, p. 107621.

Sagiroglu, S., & Sinanc, D. (2013, May). Big data: A review. In *2013 International Conference on Collaboration Technologies and Systems (CTS)*, pp. 42–47.

Selwyn, N. (2011). 'It's all about standardisation'– Exploring the digital (re)configuration of school management and administration. *Cambridge Journal of Education, 41*(4), pp. 473–488.

Sherman, E. (2015). 5 jobs that robots already are taking | Fortune. Retrieved June 16, 2020, from the website: https://fortune.com/2015/02/25/5-jobs-that-robots-already-are-taking/

Shi, C., Li, H. H., Mao, C., Shi, X., Zhang, Y., & Zhang, J. (2018). Construction and management of computer professional education laboratory in the context of big data. *Educational Sciences: Theory & Practice, 18*(6), pp. 3247–3253.

Stachowicz-Stanusch, A., & Amann, W. (2018). Artificial intelligence at universities in Poland. *Organization & Management Quarterly, 42*(2), pp. 63–82.

Ullman, S. (2019). Using neuroscience to develop artificial intelligence. *Science,* *363*(6428), pp. 692–693.

Williams, P. (2019). Does competency-based education with Blockchain signal a new mission for universities? *Journal of Higher Education Policy and Management, 41*(1), pp. 104–117.

Yang, E., & Bayapu, I. (2019). Big data analytics and facilities management: A case study. *Facilities,* 38(3/4), pp. 268–281. https://doi.org/10.1108/F-01-2019-0007

9 Embracing Artificial Intelligence in Sub-Saharan Higher Educational Institutions

James Baba Abugre

Introduction

To what extent can higher education in sub-Saharan African (SSA) be less fond of their human judgment in classroom situations instead of combining them with machine intelligence? How do educational institutions in SSA avoid the culture shock of the recent unexpected social distancing decree by many governments resulting from the COVID-19 pandemic, which has affected active teaching and learning in colleges and universities? This chapter attempts to answer these questions by supporting the recent calls of academics and social agents who have suggested the deployment of artificial intelligence (AI) and digital skills in higher educational (HE) institutions to embrace the unknown (Ehlers & Kellermann, 2019).

According to Patterson (1990), AI is a branch of computer science concerned with the study and creation of technological systems that display some form of human intelligence: a system that can learn concepts and tasks, reason, and draw useful conclusions about the world around us. For Curran and Rao (2018), AI is a collective term for computer systems that can sense their environment, think, learn, and take action in response to what they are feeling and their objectives. Curran and Rao (2018) categorized AI into four kinds. First, automated intelligence, which focuses on the automation of tasks. Second, assisted intelligence, which can help with work efficiency. Third, augmented intelligence can support the decision-making process; and fourth, autonomous intelligence, which is capable of making decisions intuitively. These automated intelligence collections depict the broad and encompassing nature of AI, making it an obligatory pipeline of competitiveness for most leading universities in today's world. Hence, industrial companies and educational institutions' business models are changing radically, and institutions must, therefore, adapt their skill set to the digital and AI world or get left behind (Sachon, 2018).

Accordingly, in the current competitive world, we are bombarded with AI's potential and its practical effect across various industries, including higher education. Research on future skills is the current hot topic of the day with fundamental job market changes due to several powerful drivers. While many studies focus on the changes brought through digital technologies, they relate future skills directly to digital skills as AI becomes more sophisticated (Ehlers & Kellermann, 2019). Consequently, educational algorithms and digital assistants are installed across most developed institutions to enhance teaching and learning diffusion. For instance, advanced technologies have been promoted to support teaching and assist in students' learning (Dyson, Vickers, Turtle, Cowan, & Tassone, 2015; Manca & Ranieri, 2017). In fact, Popenici and Kerr (2017) have argued that the future of higher education is intrinsically linked with developments in new technologies and computing capacities of the new intelligent machines. They advance the argument that in higher education, AI creates both new opportunities and challenges for teaching and learning with the power to alter the systems of governance fundamentally.

Moreover, several other studies have also illustrated how new technologies could assist with HE institutions (Brown, 2012; Dermentzi, Papagiannidis, Osorio Toro, & Yannopoulou, 2016; Hung & Yuen, 2010; Lim, Grönlund, & Andersson, 2015). For example, researching how machines can help in predicting reliable information for students to determine. Likewise, AI has now become an enhancing toolkit used by major campuses around the world daily—from internet search engines, smartphone features, and apps to classroom teaching appliances. For example, the complex set of algorithms and software that power computers and iPhone's Siri is a typical example of AI solutions that have become part of everyday experiences (Bostrom & Yudkowsky 2011; Luckin, 2017).

Despite the increase in AI-enabled applications globally, its adoption in business and higher education remains low. According to a Boston Consulting Group survey, only 1 in 20 companies globally have extensively incorporated AI, and the adoption and diffusion of AI are weak in the African continent. For example, although some 14% of the world's population reside in Africa, only 3% of the world's internet users live on the continent (Fuchs & Horak, 2008). The digital divide remains a challenge for Africa due to structural inequalities of the global network society (Fuchs & Horak, 2008). Abugre (2018) confirmed that SSA higher education has always been an infrastructure deficit that impedes their visibility in the international arena. Yet, internationalization is more characterized by digital transactions, digital users, and digitally interconnected partnerships in foreign countries (Pan & Tse, 2000), such as corporate offices, data center hubs, and international partnerships to support transnational education (UNCTAD, 2017).

The absence and deficiency of application, cultural awareness, knowledge, and usefulness of AI in HE institutions in SSA can lead to academic shock if the current craze for adopting AI and digital capabilities is overlooked. For example, the closure of all educational institutions globally due to the COVID-19 pandemic in March 2020 led to most academic institutions and lecturers in SSA experiencing anxiety, frustration, and helplessness in the new environment. The situation resulted from lacking sufficient technology to host online teaching and learning in most SSA institutions. Culture shock is defined as the degree of social difficulty encountered in a new situation when participants are not fully prepared to embrace the new environment. Higher education in SSA can adjust and avoid future shocks of technological surge if they start to embrace or catchup with the rise of innovation as digitalization and AI are setting the new rules of corporate games. More so, universities have been actively exploring the application of AI as an enabler for innovation and the advancement of higher education institutions.

Consequently, recognizing the uncertain and sometimes turbulent environment of HE institutions in SSA, this chapter explores AI's theoretical potential in assisting human-level cognition in teaching and learning and taking complex decisions in university administration's varying contexts. This chapter attempts to answer the main research question: to what extent does SSA higher education institution embrace AI technology, and would AI become the new information and communication technology (ICT) in universities in developing countries?

AI Acquisition by SSA

Global changes in the geopolitical landscape such as the COVID-19 pandemic meltdown, China–US trade impacting developing countries, Brexit, and European Union impasse have affected African countries' technology acquisition capabilities to advance their technical and market catchup. For SSA to catch up involves a greater focus on digitization, automation, and AI solutions in HE institutions and businesses are needed. Technological catchup is linked to technological leapfrogging, which supports the claim that developing countries should embrace and catch up with newer and efficient technologies such as AI rather than still depending on the older vintages of technology (Gallagher, 2006; World Bank, 2008). Technological leapfrogging inspires developing countries to speedily embrace advanced technology and avoids other means of a resource-intensive and expensive economic development form (Gallagher, 2006). With their vast natural resources, SSA countries should concentrate on advanced technology such as AI to transform them in making them competitive and marketable than focusing on their raw material, which has never benefited them over the years. Some have vigorously argued that high complexity environments are where machine learning is most useful and needed (Agrawal, Gans, & Goldfarb, 2017). With its multiethnic and multilingual complexities, SSA is critical, coupled with her vast unexploited natural resources, to embrace AI, especially in teaching and learning in her HE institutions. Advanced digitization or AI can help educational institutions structurally change university administrative services, their teaching and learning scope, and relate their computerized tasks as solutions for complex and advanced learning (Popenici & Kerr, 2017). Hence, AI has become the ICT today for many universities to embrace.

General Artificial Intelligence Usage

AI has become a sought-after phenomenon critical in supporting today's economic and social activities (Lu, Li, Chen, Kim, & Serikawa, 2018). The concept of AI has gained much recognition in recent years, as seen in many developed countries and developing countries as the key to growth and development (Acemoglu & Restrepo, 2018). Many businesses, such as information technology (IT) companies and media, have started embracing the concept of AI (Colchester, Hagras, Alghazzawi, & Aldabbagh, 2017). Nilsson (2014, p.1) described AI as a "subpart of computer science, concerned with how to give computers the sophistication to act intelligently, and to do so in increasingly wider reams." Ma and Siau (2018, p.1) also defined AI as "the ability and development of an information technology-based computer systems or other machines to compete for the tasks that usually require human intelligence and logical deduction." It is clear from the above descriptions that AI is underpinned by IT, which is indispensable to higher education.

According to Topol (2019), AI can solve many systemic errors like procedures and processes that have been detected over the years through human mistakes resulting in inefficiencies, disruption of workflows, and waste of resources. Earlier researchers such as Ford (2015) contended that AI as an advanced technology would bring about massive transformation to the world. Accordingly, it has been predicted by Forbes Technology Council that by 2030, the prospects of AI will reach $15.7 trillion in the global economy (Ma & Siau, 2018). Additionally, AI will become part and parcel of people's lives and not only belong to global business giants such as Youtube, Amazon, and so on (Siau & Wang, 2018). On their part, Siau and Yang (2017) stressed that AI and robotics would play a significant role in marketing since these technologies can automatically embark on operations. They also alluded that with AI and robotics, sales and marketing are likely to be customized in higher education commodification. The emergence of AI and robotics are fast becoming a reality, which will require professionals and academics to pay attention to the new technology (Siau & Yang, 2017). This brings to fore the importance of AI in teaching and learning. For example, merging neuroscience and AI could improve cognitive functions research and help teach medicine in medical schools (Hassabis, Kumaran, Summerfield, & Botvinick, 2017). Thus, countries and businesses will be positively influenced by AI, which impacts the global economy.

Despite these advantages, there are challenges associated with AI adoption, as researchers have identified the negative implications of AI advancement in the global economy. For instance, Baierle, Sellitto,

Frozza, Schaefer, and Habekost (2019) revealed that AI's introduction would likely throw many people out of their jobs. They further explained that most of the market jobs would be taken over by the AI machines in the future. There is a high probability that AI machines will take more human job functions (Ma & Siau, 2018). Ultimately, robotics and AI will outperform humans and consequently replace many sales and marketing professionals (Siau & Yang, 2017; Ma & Siau, 2018). However, they also contended that changes would create new jobs requiring humans and machines to work hand-in-hand. Likewise, Anum, Lodhi, and Ahmed (2018) posited that intelligent platforms and protocols developed by AI could solve knowledge management challenges. Their findings are critical as many researchers have admonished knowledge management in organizations.

Artificial Intelligence and Higher Education

Researchers have observed that AI has the potential of impacting significantly on the educational sector of countries. AI has prospects and implications for teaching and learning (Holmes, Bialik, & Fadel, 2019). There are ongoing efforts to develop AI technologies to automate all aspects of the education system, including administration, admissions, timetabling, learning management, attendance recording, and predicting students at risk of failure (Holmes, Bialik, & Fadel, 2019). From this perspective, Ma and Siau (2018) believed that AI would predominantly impact higher education areas. They indicated that AI would significantly impact the curriculum and enrollment in HE institutions of learning. The changes would result from higher speed, accuracy, and consistency of the technology on which AI was developed. Despite the advantages of AI, Ma and Siau (2018) admitted that AI technology might be deficient in soft critical skills such as critical thinking, innovation, leadership, creativity, and communication. Zamora (2018) also argued that while AI's success is numerous and still growing, AI is decades away from reaching human intelligence, if indeed, that will ever be reached. Goksel and Bozkurt (2019), in their research on AI in education, found that AI technology adoption in education would ease many activities in the educational sector, which will also go a long way to add to human advancement society. They conclude that even though AI technology is right, its adoption should not be seen without challenges. There is a need to develop a critical AI position before its adoption into the educational sector, emphasizing ethical policy for AI usage to ensure smooth adaptation of the technology in the educational sector (Goksel & Bozkurt, 2019). Vernon's (2019) research on robotics and AI in Africa identified that AI and robotics adoption in Africa's educational system is critical for Africa's growth and development. Therefore, he suggested a need for African countries to invest in AI research to help address the technology gap.

Application of Artificial Intelligence in Africa

The research reported that some African countries have seen the merit of AI and have begun adopting AI technology in banking and engineering (Issaka & Kumi-Boateng, 2020; Ukpong, Udoh, & Essien, 2019; Vernon, 2019). A study conducted on the advancement of AI identified that Africa is fast becoming aware of AI's positive impact on developing countries in which African countries are no exception (Cisse, 2018). According to him, the challenge is that most AI experts are in developed countries such as North America and Europe, whereby Africa and Asia have few experts in AI. He further explained that fewer African experts suggest opportunities to capitalize on AI to improve Africans' lives. This assertion is supported by Vernon (2019), who identified that AI and robotics could ensure the economic growth and development of developing countries. He further claimed that AI adoption in Africa would increase the effectiveness and efficiency in critical sectors such as education, health, banking, and agriculture. Issaka and Kumi-Boateng (2020) also found that geologists and geotechnical engineers in Ghana could adopt AI in monitoring tidal effects. They recommended that AI models should be used as a practical alternative technique in quantifying solid earth tides.

Challenges of Applying AI in African Universities

Adopting technology into Africa's teaching and learning process is critical to achieving success (Onyema, 2019). Despite the benefits Africa could derive from AI, it also comes with its challenges (Hao, 2019). Similarly, in a speech, Dr. Anantha Duraoappa asserted that applying AI in African universities could have some challenges (Forum on Artificial Intelligence in Africa, 2019). According to him, if the data used in training the AI system is biased, the AI will also be limited. He further indicated that AI would ignore some critical and meaningful features of students learning experience. He advised that African institutions of higher learning must identify these dangers and minimize possible bias and discrimination if they intend to adopt AI or machine learning. Adopting AI or machine learning in HE institutions comes with challenges such as huge investments and legal framework (Vernon, 2019). Higher education institutions must ensure that ethical standards regarding research and other learning processes are safeguarded. He further indicated that AI adoption in HE institutions also needs special skills, knowledge, and training currently lacking in most educational institutions. AI is fast gaining ground. Most of the tertiary institutions in Africa have no measures such as the requisite knowledge and skill system to prepare their workforce to reap the benefits (University of Pretoria, 2019). Therefore, it has advised that tertiary institutions implement the necessary measures to ensure their workers receive the requisite training to embrace emerging technology.

Also, African governments should support the tertiary institutions to provide a reliable infrastructure and a firm policy and regulatory framework to serve as a prerequisite for AI or machine learning adoption in tertiary institutions in Africa (University of Pretoria, 2019).

Empirical Approach and Insights from Experts' Narratives

This study gathered empirical data from interviews of academic administrators in a large research university in Ghana to ground this project work in the context of realism. Interviews were considered most appropriate to unearth educational administrators' reflections in their evaluation process of embracing AI as the new IT for SSA higher institutions to avoid the culture shock of being left behind in technological development. Interviews are significant as they are expressed in narratives by experts in the knowledge area. The empirical data that involved seven senior academic members who are administrators of this large university was used to situate this project's thematic position. It involved in-depth, open-ended, and mostly unstructured one-on-one interviews with the seven senior members eliciting their opinions as experts of several university administration years. The questions concerned the significance of AI and its place in teaching and learning in SSA universities. The interviewed data was subsequently transcribed and analyzed. Hence, through careful reading and thematic analysis, and categorizing the themes according to the desirability of adoption, usage merits and demerits of AI practices in current university administration in developing countries, we clustered these considerations into four groups in Figure 9.1.

Discussion of Findings

- **Adopting AI SSA Higher Education**

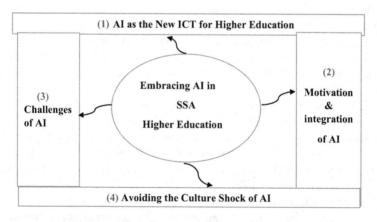

Figure 9.1 Empirical findings.

The interview findings showed that AI should be embraced as the new ICT in HE institutions in SSA. All respondents agreed that AI's importance in building a competitive global educational system in Africa is now or never. Just as IT transformed the world in accelerating today's globalization, AI should be taken as the new technology that can leapfrog the development of higher education systems. Respondents explained that AI technologies intend to reproduce human thought processes; HE institutions should develop expert pedagogical approaches that stimulate human expertise in critical thinking. Respondent # 4 echoed the issue as:

> Just as years ago, the buzz on ICT as the bedrock for developmental leapfrogging for developing countries, so is AI today for catching up on advanced technology of the developed world. So, AI is the new ICT to be embraced by developing countries if they want their universities to catch up with those of the developed world.

Equally, respondent # 6 agreed that:

> The outbreak of Covid-19 has clearly shown that universities in Africa, faculties, and students, as well as parents, are definitely rethinking the introduction of AI. In fact, African universities have not jumped but have been pushed into adopting AI in education.

- **Motivation to Embrace and Integrate AI in Higher Education in SSA**

According to the respondents, universities cannot operate without technological support in their administrative and management systems. The respondents asserted that HE institutions have been using IT systems like electronic computers and other related software programs and application tools that support these systems to give life to university operations for the past years. Therefore, introducing AI in the university system means universities update their IT systems for more significant data usage or adopting an advanced technology form. So, without a doubt, universities ought to be motivated by the significant advances in machine prediction and automation of tasks. The need to integrate advanced forms of digitization or high-tech learning and the people required to manage them should constitute the current tertiary institution's IT infrastructure. This assertion is supported and echoed by respondents # 6 and #2:

> Absolutely, AI ought to be embraced by SSA universities especially, with the issue of covid-19 and other pandemics, increasing young population, inadequate physical infrastructure, AI can play a crucial role in educational development in Africa.

The time to explore the advantages of the digital and AI landscape is now. It is imperative for university administrators to develop strategies on how to integrate AI systems to university administration.

Accordingly, all respondents agreed that there is a need for a rethinking of learning in higher education in the light of digitalization and the science of AI. The reason being that AI promises to be a powerful driver of change in HE institutions in many ways.

- **Challenges of AI Adoption in Higher Educational Institutions in SSA**

HE institutions in SSA face enormous challenges in adopting and applying AI in their teaching and learning. Most African states are in their nascent stages of development and fall within low-income countries. This makes their HE institutions lack the capacity to acquire the necessary AI science infrastructure. Moreover, the subregion is fraught with many cultural challenges that may impede her universities to directly and fully automate if not in a piecemeal manner – and this may take several years. Respondents presented a gamut of challenges of AI adoptions in Table 9.1.

- **AI Uncertainty and Culture Shock in SSA Higher Education**

Culture shock refers to the multiple demands for an adjustment that individuals or communities may experience at the cognitive, behavioral, emotional, social, and physiological levels when they are met with a new culture of doing things. Embracing AI is a culture where advanced technology adoption becomes a new way of doing things. This chapter focused on

Table 9.1 Frequency of the challenges of adoption of AI by universities

Types of challenges	R#1	R#2	R3#	R#4	R#5	R#6	R#7
AI would weaken top management's supervisory role	√			√	√	√	√
AI has ethical issues when machines cannot detect mistakes and responsibility		√		√		√	
The fear that AI would take over human jobs in SSA	√	√	√	√	√		√
African culture symbolizes human fraternity and therefore AI is a threat to livelihood	√			√	√	√	√
High cost to acquire AI and advanced digital software	√	√	√	√	√	√	√
Readiness of SSA institutions to accept and adopt AI	√		√	√		√	√

Note: R# = respondent no; √ = indication of acceptance.

integrating AI as part of the HE administrative system to accelerate university systems and processes. Almost all respondents agreed that just as the world was taken by a shock of the unexpected impact of COVID-19, so would this culture shock repeat itself on African universities in the future if they (universities in Africa) do not begin to embrace AI now. Hence, SSA HE institutions should start to embrace AI now to avoid a future culture shock. The reason being that AI promises to be a powerful driver of change to HE institutions in ways we cannot yet predict in the future to come, which was echoed strongly by respondent # 2 that:

> Technology is driving everything now, and in the not distant future, advanced technology in the form AI would drive everything in education. Students would demand the learning support that is appropriate for their situation in context. Hence, the need to embrace these advanced forms of technology is now in other not to fall into unanticipated shock.

Therefore, HE institutions in SSA must take advantage of the current craze for new IT to build a culture of innovativeness that would encourage machine learning in our universities soon. This would leapfrog the subcontinent to the demands of tomorrow's workplace, which is digitalization and machine learning.

Implications and Conclusion

The purpose of this chapter was to assess the impact and readiness of embracing AI by HE institutions in SSA. Through empirical investigation using in-depth interviews with seven senior members as experts of several years of university administration, our findings discussed their views on the advantages and qualities, including obstacles and other factors that may hinder AI uptake in HE institutions.

AI's impact is discernible in the world economy today and has captured many institutions and researchers' attention. This work demonstrates that integrating advanced technology in teaching and learning would certainly add value to the educational standards. African universities and all HE institutions must embrace the craze for human–machine interface, which can change how learning, accessing, and creating information can solve unforeseen problems, including unexpected disasters. This is very significant in the recent cases of the COVID-19 pandemic as most universities are resorting to online teaching. Hence, this work suggests that African HE institutions must seriously invest in technology and network infrastructure to facilitate learning integration. First, by embracing and integrating AI, SSA HE institutions can benefit from technological utilization, encompassing hardware and software to present educational content in the various universities. Second, by embracing and integrating AI, HE institutions can promote advanced technology for interactive online teaching and learning components in the universities. Third, by welcoming and integrating AI, HE institutions would stimulate their instructional and tutorial levels by engaging more students outside the classroom and therefore foster and facilitate effective communication in teaching.

Despite these benefits mentioned, SSA HE institutions would encounter many challenges in embracing AI, incredibly, the fact that these institutions currently lack the groundworks to embrace AI effectively. Therefore, AI adoption may face serious resistance to change as most leaders are not proactive in their dreams to develop the institutions. Second, HE institutions lack necessary logistics in advanced technology and therefore may be compelled to devote massive investment to building AI infrastructure – this can be a problem for leadership choice in terms of where to emphasize investments. This is because most African universities lack capital and depend on public funds, so government allocations and subventions may have to go to where they think in their choice, needy.

Nonetheless, the advantages and benefits of AI integration in SSA HE institutions overwhelm the few challenges that may confront them. AI will develop HE institutions and prepare them competitively to meet the demands of tomorrow's future higher education and society. This is presented in the conceptual framework as in Figure 9.2.

In conclusion, this chapter advocates for adopting advanced technologies and AI in the management and administration of higher education in SSA. The chapter suggests rethinking learning in higher education in the light of digitalization and AI to make AI a toolkit for future research and learning in SSA HE institutions. This would be a sufficient remedy to avoid the culture shock of AI during unexpected educational crises in learning institutions like the recent COVID-19 pandemic.

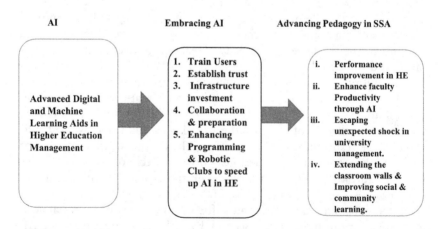

AI	Embracing AI	Advancing Pedagogy in SSA
Advanced Digital and Machine Learning Aids in Higher Education Management	1. Train Users 2. Establish trust 3. Infrastructure investment 4. Collaboration & preparation 5. Enhancing Programming & Robotic Clubs to speed up AI in HE	i. Performance improvement in HE ii. Enhance faculty Productivity through AI iii. Escaping unexpected shock in university management. iv. Extending the classroom walls & Improving social & community learning.

Figure 9.2 Conceptual framework for embracing AI in HE institutions.

References

Abugre, J. B. (2018). Institutional governance and management systems in sub-Saharan Africa higher education: Developments and challenges in a Ghanaian Research University. *Higher Education, 75*(2), pp. 323–339.

Acemoglu, D., & Restrepo, P. (2018). The race between man and machine: Implications of technology for growth, factor shares, and employment. *American Economic Review, 108*(6), pp. 1488–1542.

Agrawal, A., Gans, J., & Goldfarb, A. (2017). What to expect from artificial intelligence? *MIT Sloan Management Review, 58*(3), pp. 22–27.

Anum, L., Lodhi, S. A., & Ahmed, K. (2018). Knowledge transcendence: Strengthening knowledge management efforts on modeling transdisciplinary knowledge using artificial intelligence. *International Journal of Computer Science and Network Security, 18*(6), pp. 139–147.

Baierle, I. C., Sellitto, M. A., Frozza, R., Schaefer, J. L., & Habekost, A. F. (2019). An artificial intelligence and knowledge-based system to support the decision-making process in sales. *South African Journal of Industrial Engineering, 30*(2), pp. 17–25.

Bostrom, N., & Yudkowsky, E. (2011). The ethics of artificial intelligence. In K Frankish, W. M. Ransey (Eds.), *Cambridge Handbook of Artificial Intelligence*, (pp. 316–334). Cambridge: Cambridge University Press.

Brown, S. A. (2012). Seeing Web 2.0 in context: A study of academic perceptions. *Internet and Higher Education, 15*(1), pp. 50–57.

Cisse, M. (2018). Look to Africa to advance artificial intelligence. *Nature, 562*(7728), pp. 461–462.

Colchester, K., Hagras, H., Alghazzawi, D. and Aldabbagh, G. (2017) "A Survey of Artificial Intelligence Techniques Employed for Adaptive Educational Systems within E-Learning Platforms," *Journal of Artificial Intelligence and Soft Computing Research, 7*(1), pp. 47–64.

Curran, C., & Rao, A. (2018.) "Briefing: Artificial intelligence," PwC: Next in Tech (blog), accessed April 17, 2019, http://usblogs.pwc.com/emerging-technology/briefing-ai/.

Dermentzi, E., Papagiannidis, S., Osorio Toro, C., & Yannopoulou, N. (2016). Academic engagement: Differences between intention to adopt social networking sites and other online technologies. *Computers in Human Behavior, 61*, pp. 321–332.

Dyson, B., Vickers, K., Turtle, J., Cowan, S., & Tassone, A. (2015). Evaluating the use of Facebook to increase student engagement and understanding in lecture-based classes. *Higher Education, 69*(2), pp. 303–313.

Ehlers, U. -D., & Kellermann, S. A. (2019). *Future Skills – The Future of Learning and Higher Education. Results of the International Future Skills Delphi Survey*. Karlsruhe: Baden Wurttemberg-Cooperative State University.

Ford, M. (2015). *Rise of the Robots: Technology and the Threat of a Jobless Future*. New York: Basic Books.

Forum on Artificial Intelligence in Africa (2019). Retrieved from https://en.unesco.org/sites/default/files/participants_10_12_pdf.pdf

Fuchs, C., & Horak, E. (2008). Africa and the digital divide. *Telematics and Information, 25*(2), pp. 99–116.

Gallagher, K. S. (2006). Limits to leapfrogging in energy technologies? Evidence from the Chinese automobile industry. Energy Policy, 34, pp. 383–394.

Goksel, N., & Bozkurt, A. (2019). Artificial intelligence in education: Current insights and future perspectives. In *Handbook of Research on Learning in the Age of Transhumanism* (pp. 224–236). IGI Global: Nil Goksel and Aras Bozkurt.

Hao K. (2019, June 21). *The Future of AI Research Is in Africa*. Retrieved from www.technologyreview.com/2019/06/21/134820/ai-africa-machine-learning-ibm-google/

Hassabis, D., Kumaran, D., Summerfield, C., & Botvinick, M. (2017). Neuroscience-inspired artificial intelligence. *Neuron, 95*(2), pp. 245–258.

Holmes, W., Bialik, M., & Fadel, C. (2019). *Artificial Intelligence in Education: Promises and Implications for Teaching and Learning*. Boston, MA: Center for Curriculum Redesign.

Hung, H. T., & Yuen, S. C. Y. (2010). Educational use of social networking technology in higher education. *Teaching in Higher Education, 15*(6), pp. 703–714.

Issaka, Y., & Kumi-Boateng, B. (2020). Artificial intelligence techniques for predicting tidal effects based on geographic locations in Ghana. *Geodesy and Cartography, 46*(1), pp. 1–7.

Lim, N., Grönlund, Å., & Andersson, A. (2015). Cloud computing: The beliefs and perceptions of Swedish school principals. *Computers and Education, 84*, pp. 90–100.

Lu, H., Li, Y., Chen, M., Kim, H., & Serikawa, S. (2018). Brain intelligence: Go beyond artificial intelligence. *Mobile Networks and Applications, 23*(2), pp. 368–375.

Luckin, R. (2017). Towards artificial intelligence-based assessment systems. *Nature Human Behaviour, 1*(0028), pp. 1–3. doi: 10.1038/s41562-016-0028.

Ma, Y., & Siau, K. L. (2018). Artificial intelligence impacts on higher education. *MWAIS Proceedings, 42*(5), pp. 1–5.

Manca, S., & Ranieri, M. (2017). Implications of social network sites for teaching and learning. Where we are and where we want to go. *Education and Information Technologies, 22*(2), pp. 605–622.

Nilsson, N. J. (2014). *Principles of Artificial Intelligence*. San Francisco, CA: Morgan Kaufmann.

Onyema, E. M. (2019). Integration of emerging technologies in teaching and learning process in Nigeria: The challenges. *Central Asian Journal of Mathematical Theory and Computer Sciences, 1*(1), pp. 35–39.

Pan, Y., & Tse, D. K. (2000). The hierarchical model of market entry modes. *Journal of International Business Studies, 31*(4), pp. 535–554.

Patterson, D. W. (1990). *Introduction to Artificial Intelligence and Expert Systems*. New Delhi: Prentice-Hall of India.

Popenici, S. A., & Kerr, S. (2017). Exploring the impact of artificial intelligence on teaching and learning in higher education. *Research and Practice in Technology Enhanced Learning, 12*(1), pp. 1–13.

Sachon, M. (2018). The building blocks of Industry 4.0. *IESE Alumni Magazine*, Jan–March, p. 24.

Siau, K., & Wang, W. (2018). Building trust in artificial intelligence, machine learning, and robotics. *Cutter Business Technology Journal, 31*(2), pp. 47–53.

Siau, K., & Yang, Y. (2017, May). Impact of artificial intelligence, robotics, and machine learning on sales and marketing. Twelve Annual Midwest Association for Information Systems Conference (MWAIS 2017) (pp. 18–19). Springfield, IL, USA.

Topol, E. J. (2019). High-performance medicine: The convergence of human and artificial intelligence. *Nature Medicine, 25*(1), pp. 44–56.

UNCTAD (2017). *World Investment Report 2017: Investment and the Digital Economy.* New York and Geneva: United Nations.

Ukpong, E. G., Udoh, I. I., & Essien, I. T. (2019). Artificial intelligence: Opportunities, issues and applications in banking, accounting, and auditing in Nigeria. *Asian Journal of Economics, Business and Accounting, 10*(1): pp. 1–6.

University of Pretoria (2019, March 27). *Artificial Intelligence for Africa: An Opportunity for Growth, Development, and Democratisation.* Retrieved from www.up.ac.za/media/shared/7/ZP_Files/ai-forafrica.zp165664.pdf.

Vernon, D. (2019). Robotics and artificial intelligence in Africa [Regional]. *IEEE Robotics & Automation Magazine, 26*(4), pp. 131–135.

World Bank. (2008). Global Economic Prospects: Technology Diffusion in the Developing World. Washington, DC: Author.

Zamora, J. (2018). Artificial Intelligence, Real leadership. *IESE Business School Insight*, Fall, p. 20.

Part IV

Management Education and Automation

10 Envisioning the Future of Management Education

Hamid H. Kazeroony

Introduction

The required changes in the management education to address automation necessitate building on what we have captured in previous chapters and review the universal view of the society, the current state of industrial paradigm, the concepts of work, office environment, and the required skills. First, we will review what others have already discussed about society, the new industrial revolution (4IR), changing work environment, office work, and skill sets. Second, we assess how each layer, the society, the industrial revolution, work, office, and the required skill has changed. Finally, we propose a set of recommendations for management education to address the necessary skill sets and competencies for their students to be employable.

Society, 4IR, Management Education, and Employability

Kazeroony, in Chapter 1, explained why there is a need to reexamine societal changes and changes in the industrial paradigm and present alternatives to the current management education for making graduates employable in the future. Murayama, in Chapter 2 suggested, using the Japanese example, focusing on the acceleration of digital and robotic integration to improve productivity in meeting sustainability goals. Nyagadza, in Chapter 3, pointed out that 4IR will change the nature and dynamics of teachers and learners due to the rise of robotics and artificial intelligence (AI) in the automation of higher education. In Chapter 4, Sato outlined the rise of predictive analytics through various connected gadgets, the lack of attention to robotics' ethical requirements, and the feeling of alienation that has affected individuals. Sato argued that the three issues must be resolved by management education as we move forward. In Chapter 5, Ellis defined how organizations must changing their training and development to engage and retain GenZ employees, using AI learning, fundamentally shifting their training paradigm, which implied the need for management education to change to help facilitate this process. In Chapter 6, Aleksander, using an example from Poland, addressed the economic firms' demand for reinvestment in response to Industry 4.0. Aleksander argued that as companies require rapid changes, they need talented leaders who can balance the ethical consideration for new Industry 4.0 dynamics with the necessary technical competences. In Chapter 7, Masood expounded Ellis's definition further, stating that management education must produce employable graduates with a cross-disciplinary perspective and practice-based education based on market needs, using work-immersion through the integration of work with learning or through simulations. In Chapter 8, Damoah and Baku, using the Ghanaian example, showed how technological disparities and regulation could impact learning as we move forward. Expanding on Damoah and Baku, in Chapter 9, Abugre, using sub-Saharan Africa, argued that lack of the necessary logistics and resources, despite best intentions, will compound the regional disparities in technology adaptation in some parts of the world. Abugre explained that the lack of the necessary infrastructure would deprive learners of acquiring the required competencies and skills to compete effectively in obtaining employment.

Connecting the Changes to Employability

Turning our attention to societal and industrial paradigm changes, we examine how Society 5.0 is connected to the Fourth Industrial Revolution (4IR), leading to new social, political, economic, and technological relationships, enabling global citizens to achieve the UN's sustainability goals needed for new skill sets by management education graduate. Society 5.0 is described as combining technology and smart society's creativity to include problem-solving and value creation leading to sustainable development (World Economic Forum, 2019). Society 5.0 builds on 4IR, using local creativity to achieve UN 17 sustainability goals (United Nations, n.d.).

Society 5.0 is a temporal place where society operates cashless. In some societies, only 13% of transactions are by cash, while in others, coins are in the process of elimination from circulation, and in almost all large transactions, cash plays no part (Fabris, 2019). A cashless society required highly developed technology to replace money with digital accounting would eliminate the shadow economy as we know it and would dismantle the current criminal enterprises, replacing them with new digital forms (Fabris, 2019).

Society 5.0 is arriving at the Holocene period, facing an ecological quandary (Saijo, 2018). The future society must change its relationship with the environment to preserve its continued existence requiring new economic, social, and political order to overcome technological challenges for living in harmony with nature (Saijo, 2018). Society 5.0 would be radically shifted from its present conditions, requiring exponentially more sophisticated programming, interconnecting arts, sciences, social activities, and every imaginable facet of life (Dufva & Dufva, 2019). Society

5.0, some argue, may transition to the liberation of subalterns, decolonizing the minds, equalizing the South and the North, requiring new collective social and economic dynamics (Tilzey, 2017). Therefore, Society 5.0 requires adaptation of 4IR to ecological concern for sustainability, including equity in its fabrics, adjusting for new work, workspace, and new competencies by the management education graduates to respond to them.

The Fourth Industrial Revolution (4IR) has been defined and characterized by the remote production of services and products. Massive labor displacement would create more income inequality due to massive robotics use (Schwab, 2016). 4IR has been described to create more connectivity, social polarization and vanishing middle-class, the exponential increase in disruptive technologies, drastic improvement in the supply chain, creation of on-demand manufacturing, the convergence of physical, biological, and technological world with more connectivity to immediate policymaking by citizens in their respective governments, the need for balancing individual privacy, information, and connectivity (Schwab, 2016). The 4IR has changed the work, workspace, educational setting, dynamics, and the new requirements for employability by management education graduates.

The Fourth Industrial Revolution (4IR) has created new work dynamics based on the relation between robots and people, workspace, and opportunities. First, we examine work, work dynamics, and workspace and their impact on new management education graduates' employability requirements. Several factors have changed the concepts of work and workspace. Work has become human-centric with the man–machine interface to enhance human cognitive abilities, technology-oriented, where machines interface to complete many routine tasks, and community-oriented where service mediated interaction between organizations occurs (Anya, Nagar, & Tawfik, 2011). As far back as 2003, the nature of work changed because of technology integration, scalability, and ease of access (Stevens, Papka, & Disz, 2003). The introduction of new technologies such as three-dimensional aerial image interface has made the remote meetings close to physical presence connectivity a possibility, changing workspaces (Matsumaru, Septiana, & Horiuchi, 2019). As businesses look to minimize expense and improve productivity, the technology they utilize to reduce space expenditure, using remote connectivity (Bradley & Woodling, 2000). In regions such as northern Europe, while the office hierarchy has flattened based on historical, cultural, and connectivity, office space has become more individualistic, catering to different working needs (Nenonen, & Lindahl, 2017). Work has evolved to be a set of activities rather than a particular space where employees complete work (McGregor, 2000).

The Fourth Industrial Revolution has ushered in a slew of changes to management education. As of 2016, over 30% of students had taken at least one online class; the pedagogical model has changed to include interactivity between student-automated system-instructors, adaptive learning using computer-assisted programming has been incorporated into instruction, and the interactions between student and the instructor have been minimized (Picciano, 2019). With the development of super-computing, AI, robotics, and biosensing devised, underlined by nano-technology and quantum computing, management education moves in a new direction (Picciano, 2019). As this work goes to publication, we do not know precisely how the pivoting from face-to-face teaching to online and reliance on technology due to the COVID-19 pandemic has fundamentally changed education's nature. However, if the telltale signs are any indications, it is not easy to imagine that we would revert to what higher education was in the past. To assess the impact and provide some guidance about the future of management education and the role of auto-mation, we also need to examine how the recent COVID-19 pandemic has changed work nature.

Like the industrial revolution of the 19th century, rapid automation and disruptive technologies would lead to workers' displacement at the social and political level. The displacement of workers requires polit-ical leaders to redesign higher education policies, enabling dislocated workers to find new jobs based on exponential technology changes (Rani & Grimshaw, 2019). Reimagining higher education, first, we must con-sider its integration into Society 5.0. Therefore, higher education crit-ical success factors such as "as tradition, image, location, infrastructure, marketing, services, faculty qualification, method, cost/benefit, and library" must be reenvisioned (Panizzon & Barcellos, 2020, p. 413). Universities must become agile, responding to ecological needs for sus-tainability and disruptive technologies rather than taking two years to complete their review process for creating a new program (Panizzon & Barcellos, 2020, p. 413). Others have already made several predictions and recommendations, based on what we already know, about the future of higher education in general and management education.

Both service and manufacturing have fundamentally changed, pointing at different types of employees in the future. In service industries, the distributed operating system, the embedded devices, virtualization of operating system layers, and mobile devices have been exploited to create a virtual environment, building a community of employees serving their clients (Schubert et al., 2009). In manufacturing, the predictive analytics algorithm will allow for robust interaction and coordination of human employees and robotics in the future (Zanchettin et al., 2019). Therefore, the future employee requires different skill sets to work in a different office space, various technological competencies, and work in coordin-ation with robotics. The future employee requires different management education to work in an automated world.

To envision a future management education, we must first understand the nature of jobs and future employees. Careers such as psychologists may remain because people will still suffer from stress and other life challenges. However, the discipline must teach psychology from a different perspective to enable the psychologist to understand new life challenges such as stress caused by working with robots. The same principle applies to management education where the office environment, virtualization of operating systems, working with robots, and new office format require a different skill set. Automation requires management education to reframe itself in preparing its graduates to manage a space mining operation or work with AI to manage defense departments or reconstruct ecosystems for sustainability (Neagu, 2020).

Management education requires different ways of educating its students. First, it should provide a collaborative synchronous learning environment offering students work-based learning projects, coaching students with hints, and showing the way (Constantino-Gonzales & Suthers, 2003). Second, it should integrate sociotechnical skills in its curriculum for its future graduates. Management education should use virtualized operating systems, predictive analytics, aggregate data, ratification intelligence, and adaptive technologies to envision what to teach, how to teach, and where to teach to align its graduates' skills with the market needs (Macgilchrist, Allert, & Bruch, 2020). Third, management education should decenter itself, disengaging social stratification embedded in teacher-learner interaction, allowing learners to create their learning without cultural constraints (Thomas, 2018). Fourth, management education using augmented disruptive technologies must inculcate a digital mindset in its graduates, enabling them to be employable in a continually changing workplace. Fifth, consistent with the UN's sustainability goals, management education should restructure its curricula to include pure humanism (United Nations, n.d.). Management education can meet pure humanism objectives by promoting human dignity, common good, co-creation, self-management, refocusing the curricula on reflection, positive psychology, social entrepreneurship, and transformative changemakers experiences (Herrmann & Rundshagen, 2020).

What Is not Working

As we have discussed throughout various chapters and as others have addressed, we face a management education at higher education institutions that is in an untenable position for delivering the type of employable graduates who can work in the current or future workplace.

A Gallup poll from 2014 revealed that 96% of chief academic officers say that they are very or somewhat useful in preparing students for future employment. In contrast, business leaders in a separate study said that only 34% of the students they get from universities are ready for work (Estrada-Worthington, 2015).

In 2011, I explained that higher education institutions were operating in silos and did not realize the impact of digitization on education and its significance in making their graduates employable (Kazeroony, 2011).

The case was evident as the COVID-19 pandemic was spreading around the globe in 2020. Lack of preparedness was manifested in several areas. First, a lack of attention and resources for integrating technology into teaching and learning was apparent when reassessing the students' access to online classrooms with inadequate infrastructure. Second, the faculty worldwide felt stranded without sufficient technology to create learning communities for their students. Third, the faculty lacked enough visions into providing learning insights for their students to think independently and form knowledge from the communicated information. However, technological challenges are only one part of what is not working. Equally important, there was a lack of attention to other significant societal and ecological shortcomings, causing additional challenges for future management education graduates.

Various international bodies have recognized several issues requiring management educators' attention. United Nations (n.d.) outlined 17 sustainability goals imperative to our global community's health, ranging from the environment to how we treat each other as individuals. Other international bodies such as OECD and European Economic Community have outlined similar challenges that require addressing in management education to prepare the graduates for employability (Succi & Cinque, 2015).

Pathway Forward for Management Education in the Age of Automation

Institutions must reset their approach to management education by adopting the following recommendations:

1 Create mandatory management education councils in coordination with industries to:
   a Assess the competences required for managing with a forward-looking perspective, revising new curricula, testing them, and revising the current curricula continually (Blass & Hayward, 2015).
   b Develop curricula based on the industries' need and in compliance with the UN Principles for Responsible Management Education (United Nations, 2021) and UN 17 sustainability goals (United Nations, n.d.).
2 Develop the faculty to evaluate the unfolding disruptive social and technological structures, recognize their profession's peculiarities, and mastering the cultural, technical, and pedagogical path forward (Agranovich et al., 2019).
3 Retain a focus on soft skills such as creative and critical thinking for problem-solving, decision-making, interpersonal and intercultural communication, and dealing with stress and emotions (Succi & Cinque, 2015).

4 Prepare their management graduates to function in Society 5.0, Industry 4.0, interacting with robots and people, recognizing their ethical responsibility in working with robotics, people, and developing new AI.

References

Agranovich, Y., Amirova, A., Ageyeva, L., Lebedeva, L., Aldibekova, S., & Uaidullakyzy, E. (2019). The formation of self-organizational skills of student's academic activity on the basis of "time management" technology. *International Journal of Emerging Technologies in Learning*, 14(22), pp. 95–110.

Anya, O., Nagar, A., & Tawfik, H. (2011). Building adaptive systems for collaborative e-work: The e-Workbench approach. *Intelligent Decision Technologies*, 5(1), pp. 83–100.

Blass, E., & Hayward, P. (2015). Developing globally responsible leaders: What role for business schools in the future? *Futures*, 66, pp. 35–44.

Bradley, S., & Woodling, G. (2000). Accommodating future business intelligence new workspace and worktime challenges for management and design. *Facilities*, 18(3–4), pp. 162–167.

Constantino-Gonzales, M. A., & Suthers, D. D. (2003, January). Automated coaching of collaboration based on workspace analysis: Evaluation and implications for future learning environments. In *Proceedings of the 36th Annual Hawaii International Conference on System Sciences* (pp. 10–pp). IEEE.

Dufva, T., & Dufva, M. (2019). Grasping the future of the digital society. *Futures*, 107, pp. 17–28.

Estrada-Worthington, R. (2015). GMAC viewpoints: The future of graduate management education and how schools can prepare students for the next decade. *Graduate Management News*, p. 6.

Fabris, N. (2019). Cashless society – The future of money or a utopia? *Journal of Central Banking Theory and Practice*, 8(1), pp. 53–66.

Herrmann, B., & Rundshagen, V. (2020). Paradigm shift to implement SDG 2 (end hunger): A humanistic management lens on the education of future leaders. *The International Journal of Management Education*, 18(1), pp. 1–13.

Kazeroony, H. (2011). *Strategic Management of Higher Education: Serving students as Customers for Institutional Growth*. New York, NY: Business Expert Press.

Macgilchrist, F., Allert, H., & Bruch, A. (2020). Students and society in the 2020s. Three future "histories" of education and technology. *Learning, Media and Technology*, 45(1), pp. 76–89.

Matsumaru, T., Septiana, A. I., & Horiuchi, K. (2019). Three-dimensional aerial image interface, 3DAII. *Journal of Robotics and Mechatronics*, 31(5), pp. 657–670.

McGregor, W. (2000). The future of workspace management. *Facilities*, 18(3/4), pp. 138–143.

Neagu, S. N. (2020). The future jobs in a technological society. *eLearning & Software for Education*, 2, pp. 603–609.

Nenonen, S. P., & Lindahl, G. (2017). Nordic workplace concept development from office as a city to city as an office. *Journal of Facilities Management*, 15(3), pp. 302–316.

Panizzon, M., & Barcellos, P. F. P. (2020). Critical success factors of the university of the future in a Society 5.0: A maturity model. *World Future Review (Sage Publications Inc.)*, *12*(4), pp. 410–426.

Picciano, A. G. (2019). Artificial intelligence and the academy's loss of purpose. *Online Learning*, *23*(3), pp. 270–284.

Rani, U., & Grimshaw, D. (2019). Introduction: What does the future promise for work, employment and society? *International Labour Review*, *158*(4), pp. 577–592.

Saijo, T. (2018). Future design: Bequeathing sustainable natural environments and sustainable societies to future generations. *Social Design Engineering Series*, *23*, pp. 64–67.

Schwab, K. (January 14, 2016). [The Fourth Industrial Revolution: What It Means, How to Respond]. Retrieved December 25, 2020, www.weforum.org

Schubert, L., Kipp, A., Koller, B., & Wesner, S. (2009). Service-oriented operating systems: Future workspaces. *IEEE Wireless Communications*, *16*(3), pp. 42–50.

Stevens, R., Papka, M. E., & Disz, T. (2003). Prototyping the workspaces of the future. *IEEE Internet Computing*, *7*(4), pp. 51–58.

Succi, C., & Cinque, M. (2015). Hard findings on soft skills. *Annual International Conference on Tourism & Hospitality Research*, pp. 45–52.

Thomas, H. (2018). Powerful knowledge, technology and education in the future-focused good society. *Technology in Society*, *52*, pp. 54–59.

Tilzey, M. (2017). Reintegrating economy, society, and environment for cooperative futures: Polanyi, Marx, and food sovereignty. *Journal of Rural Studies*, *53*, pp. 317–334.

United Nations (n.d.). [UN Sustainable Development Goals] [Fact sheet]. UN Sustainable Development Goals. Retrieved December 25, 2020, from www.un.org/sustainabledevelopment/

United Nations (2021). *PRME Principles for Responsible Management Education*. Retrieved January 2, 2021, from www.unprme.org

World Economic Forum (2019). *HR4.0: Shaping People Strategies in the Fourth Industrial Revolution*. www3.weforum.org/docs/WEF_NES_Whitepaper_HR4.0.pdf

Zanchettin, A. M., Casalino, A., Piroddi, L., & Rocco, P. (2019). Prediction of human activity patterns for human–robot collaborative assembly tasks. *IEEE Transactions on Industrial Informatics*, *15*(7), p. 3934.

Index

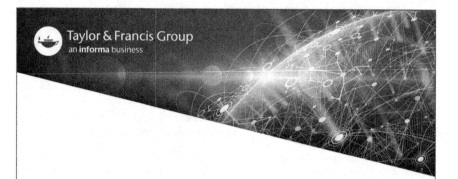

Taylor & Francis eBooks

www.taylorfrancis.com

A single destination for eBooks from Taylor & Francis
with increased functionality and an improved user
experience to meet the needs of our customers.

90,000+ eBooks of award-winning academic content in
Humanities, Social Science, Science, Technology, Engineering,
and Medical written by a global network of editors and authors.

TAYLOR & FRANCIS EBOOKS OFFERS:

A streamlined
experience for
our library
customers

A single point
of discovery
for all of our
eBook content

Improved
search and
discovery of
content at both
book and
chapter level

REQUEST A FREE TRIAL
support@taylorfrancis.com

Printed in the United States
by Baker & Taylor Publisher Services